CINDERELLA & THE GLASS CEILING

CINDERELLA
& THE GLASS
CEILING

AND OTHER
FEMINIST
FAIRY TALES

A PARODY

LAURA LANE & ELLEN HAUN

ILLUSTRATED BY NICOLE MILES

SEAL PRESS

NEW YORK

Seal Press

Hachette Book Group

1290 Avenue of the Americas, New York, NY 10104

www.sealpress.com

@sealpress

Printed in the United States of America

First Edition: March 2020

Published by Seal Press, an imprint of Perseus Books, LLC, a subsidiary of Hachette Book Group, Inc. The Seal Press name and logo is a trademark of the Hachette Book Group.

The Hachette Speakers Bureau provides a wide range of authors for speaking events. To find out more, go to www.hachettespeakersbureau.com or call (866) 376-6591.

The publisher is not responsible for websites (or their content) that are not owned by the publisher.

Illustrated by Nicole Miles

Print book interior design by Ann Kirchner

Library of Congress Cataloging-in-Publication Data
Names: Lane, Laura, author. | Haun, Ellen, author. | Miles, Nicole, illustrator.
Title: Cinderella & the glass ceiling: and other feminist fairy tales: a parody / Laura Lane, Ellen Haun; illustrated by Nicole Miles.
Other titles: Cinderella and the glass ceiling
Description: First edition. | New York: Seal Press, 2020.
Identifiers: LCCN 2019044878 | ISBN 9781580059060 (board) | ISBN 9781580059053 (ebook)
Subjects: LCSH: Fairy tales—Adaptations. | Feminist fiction, American.
Classification: LCC PS3612.A54985 A6 2020 | DDC 818/.602—dc23
LC record available at https://lccn.loc.gov/2019044878

ISBNs: 978-1-58005-906-0 (paper over board), 978-1-58005-905-3 (ebook)

LSC-W

10 9 8 7 6 5 4 3 2 1

*For Rilo. You were in my belly when
we started writing and on my lap when
we finished. May you and all other
babies read fairy tales that don't suck.*

For Mom. Thank you.

CONTENTS

INTRODUCTION

NCE UPON A TIME...
Fairy tales were patriarchal horror stories masked as children's tales. A woman had to cook and clean for her seven male roommates. A wolf stalked a young girl and then committed a home invasion and double homicide. A woman fell in love with her hairy captor. A mermaid gave up her voice, friends, and family for a stranger with a sailboat. A snobby girl broke into and entered a family's home and ate their breakfast. A man-child who refused to grow up sat in a window creeping on children. Multiple men kissed sleeping women without their consent. Oh, and nearly everyone was depicted as white.

These stories were full of beasts, villains, and judgy mirrors. But the worst enemy of all? Other women. Nothing was scarier than a woman over thirty out to get you!

Stepmothers, stepsisters, witches, fairies, and sea monsters—they were always portrayed as evil. They were all unhappily single. And a lot of them had widows' peaks. They either wanted to steal your inheritance and make you sleep in a fireplace or murder you for being too hot.

Women were never nuanced in these stories. There were only two types: evil (too much purple eye shadow) and good (over-plucked brows). Every once in a while you got a mouse thrown in there who happened to be female, but all she really did was sew.

In these stories, women were taught they should do anything to marry a rich dude, preferably a prince. All they needed to do to land the guy was have really good hair and a need to get rescued. Once they got the guy and defeated the Evil Other Woman out to get them, their story was over. They didn't have much agency. They weren't empowered. And they never had a female friend to vent to!

Terrifying, no?

But just as we don't wear neck ruffs anymore, times have changed, and so should these stories. (Seriously though, we hope wearing a fan around your neck never makes a comeback.)

In our fairy tales, women get the last word on their own terms. They know the only thing cooler than a mermaid tail is a vagina. They know they have to work a lot harder to break the glass ceiling than a glass slipper. And they know that happily ever after is a myth created by the patriarchy.

THE LITTLE MERMAID GETS A VAGINA

NCE UPON A TIME...
There lived a bold and curious young mermaid with her father and many mermaid sisters in a palace deep under the sea and far away from the damage of oil spills, plastic straws, and humans who pee in the ocean. She had everything she needed, but the Mermaid yearned for something more. She wanted to explore, but mostly she wanted to hang out with hot sailors.

Despite the warnings of her overbearing father not to go to the surface, where she could potentially get harpooned by fishermen, she would swim up and gawk at the humans on boats. (She would later in life realize her father was completely reasonable and doing his best to deal with a rebellious teenager.) She became particularly taken with one sailor, who was predictably a prince.

After following the Prince's boat around for a few nights and acting like a total groupie, she made the choice: she wanted to go on land permanently. She wanted to become a human and make out with the hot sailor Prince.

The Mermaid set out to find the Sea Witch, who supported her expensive micro-scale-abrasion habit by securing realistic-looking fake IDs and casting magical spells for desperate mermen.

"I want to become a human," the Mermaid said to the Sea Witch. "I want legs. I want platform sandals. I want that hot sailor ass."

"My dear, sweet teenybopper mermaid, that's what I do," said the Sea Witch. "I live to help impulsive, unfortunate, hormonal merfolk. In exchange for my services, I'll need something in return. Don't worry, I don't want your allowance. What I want is just a trifle . . . your voice. Also, you can never come back."

The Mermaid didn't use her voice much under the sea anyway, since most sea creatures were highly evolved and communicated by jamming on shell drums. Plus, she could always write the Prince a note if she needed to tell him something. Leaving her family, on the other fin, was a big deal. But sometimes when you're crushing hard, you don't think too straight and you do stupid shit.

"I'm in!" said the Mermaid.

And with that, she signed the contract. It immediately turned into a soggy inky mess since paper doesn't do well under water.

The Mermaid closed her eyes and waited nervously for the transformation to begin. She waited. And she waited. But nothing happened. She peeked out of one eye.

"How long does this legs thing take?" she asked the Sea Witch.

The Sea Witch took a deep breath. "Actually, we need to discuss something first."

"Is it about my legs?" asked the Mermaid.

"Kinda. I have to give you 'the talk.' You see, along with the legs, you also get . . . a vagina."

The Mermaid was confused.

"A vagina-ma-bob?"

"It's just called a vagina."

The Mermaid didn't want any extra stuff with this deal. She had only requested the legs, after all.

"I only want legs, thanks," said the Mermaid, swimming over to the Sea Witch so she would hopefully get a move on with this legs spell already.

"There's no work-around. I've tried before. Peeing out of the mouth was very gross."

"Let's just get to the legs. I'm sure I can figure out my vagina on my own," she said, rather impatiently.

"Listen, sweetie, vaginas are complicated. I'm not going to let you walk away with a pussy you don't know how to use."

The Mermaid looked at the Sea Witch. Was this some sort of trick? Sure, she pretty much trusted the Sea Witch or else she wouldn't have come to her in the first place. But she had heard a rumor about a time the Sea Witch turned a merman requesting hair plugs into a catfish.

"Why are you being nice to me? Aren't you evil?" asked the Mermaid.

"Here's the thing, I'm a Sea Witch who looks out for myself. But we're both still fighting the mermantriarchy, right? So as they say on land: Girl Code."

The Sea Witch patted a rock nearby, gesturing for the Mermaid to sit down for the talk.

"First things first: periods," said the Sea Witch, holding up a red piece of sea anemone as a prop. "Once a month your vagina will bleed for about a week."

"Is it injured?" asked the Mermaid.

"Nope, that's normal and perfectly healthy. It will be extremely painful and it will happen until you're about fifty."

The Sea Witch quietly snickered to herself.

The Mermaid began to have second thoughts. "If I had known the vagina was part of the deal I would have thought this through a little harder."

"But remember, with legs you can walk and run and do squats," said the Sea Witch.

Ooo squats! So fun. The Mermaid got up from the rock and tried to do a squat, only to discover you can't do squats with a tail.

"I want to squat more than anything!" said the Mermaid. "I can deal with periods. Thank you for having the talk. I'm ready for the legs."

"Oh dear, sweet Mermaid, we're just getting started," said the Sea Witch, pointing to the rock and motioning to sit the fuck back down. "Vaginas are also used for sex. If you're having sex with a man, which the Prince is, you're basically shoving his penis repeatedly into your vagina for like ten minutes, give or take."

The Sea Witch mimed a thrusting penis using a loose piece of coral and a conch shell. The Mermaid was horrified.

"Does that feel good?" asked the Mermaid.

"Sometimes. But you'll need to take this."

The Sea Witch pulled out a pack of birth control pills from her bosom and handed it to the Mermaid. The Mermaid opened the small plastic compact with tiny pills inside, took one out, and studied it. She believed she was very skilled when it came to figuring out how to use human inventions. She had years of practice from collecting other shipwrecked treasures under the sea.

"A human nose plug gadget!" the Mermaid exclaimed as she stuck a pill in her nose.

The Sea Witch shook her head. "This is why they give women sugar pills for a week," she mumbled to herself.

"That's a type of birth control. It will fix your face acne," explained the Sea Witch. "But it will make you bloated and depressed."

The Mermaid blew the birth control out of her nose.

"No, thank you," said the Mermaid. "No birth control, no legs for me."

But the Sea Witch was convincing.

"Imagine being able to jump and skip and ride a stationary bike that doesn't go anywhere!"

"That sounds so fun!" said the Mermaid. "Okay, fine. I'll use birth control-whose-it and I'll deal with the water weight."

"Great. You'll also want to make sure the Prince puts this on," said the Sea Witch as she pulled out a condom and handed it to the Mermaid.

The Mermaid studied the plastic square the size of a small seashell and ripped it open.

"I am really good at knowing what to do with land objects," bragged the Mermaid. "This is clearly that sticky stuff humans chew and then throw on the ground for someone else to step on."

She promptly stuffed the condom into her mouth.

"Thith ith thomething for my collethion," said the Mermaid with her mouth full. "I'll call ith a whatz-it-gum-lore!"

The Sea Witch stared at her, letting time pass longer than it needed to.

"You put that on his dick," said the Sea Witch, finally.

The Mermaid spat it out, but tried to play it cool.

"Yeah, yeah, yeah, I know that," said the Mermaid as she wiped some of the slimy lubricant off her mouth.

"You'll wanna make sure he uses that," explained the Sea Witch. "The Prince is a sailor, so he definitely has syphilis and genital warts. He won't talk about it, so it's been untreated for years. STI-shaming is a big problem on land."

That was all the Mermaid needed to hear to change her mind once again.

"Come to think of it, I barely know him," she said, realizing that maybe the Prince wasn't as cute as she remembered. "So I'm not sure I need the legs anymore."

"But don't you want to be able to dance and spin and one day have a human child?" asked the Sea Witch.

The Mermaid whipped her head around. She hadn't even thought about having a human child! She'd seen photos in the shipwrecks but had never seen one in merperson.

"A baby-gizmo!" cried the Mermaid.

"Do you know where the baby-gizmo comes out of?" asked the Sea Witch.

The Mermaid thought about it. There was most definitely only one hole large enough for a baby to possibly come out of.

The Mermaid smiled and announced, "Your mouth!"

"That's a hard no," said the Sea Witch. "Your vagina."

Hmmm. Maybe vaginas weren't how she was picturing them after all.

"So vaginas are big, like the size of a flounder?"

"No. They're small. Like half a lobster."

Oh dear Poseidon. Vaginas were exactly how she pictured them after all.

"How does that work?" asked the Mermaid, not sure if she wanted to know the answer.

"It really doesn't. A chunk of the time they cut the gizmo out of you. And when that doesn't happen, the baby will rip apart your vagina, tearing it from vagina to anus. You'll feel like you're dying. The whole situation could become one big butthole!"

This was all the Mermaid needed to hear to back out once and for all. She slowly floated backward away from the Sea Witch and toward the exit of the lair, trying hard not to make it too obvious that she was ready to make a swim for it.

"You know," she said as she got farther and farther away. "The more I think about it, I'm very happy under the sea. There's plenty of scaly pop stars for me to obsess over down here instead. Tails aren't so bad. I appreciate your time but I've changed my mind. No deal!"

But it was too late.

"Honey, you signed the contract!" roared the Sea Witch, holding up the soggy, yet still visible, contract.

"Bwahahahahahaha!"

The Sea Witch laughed ominously as smoke billowed around the Mermaid. She felt her tail melting beneath her and transforming into legs.

The Human Formerly Known as Mermaid quickly began to doggy-kick her way to the surface of the ocean. No longer able to speak or breathe underwater, she could feel her heart in her throat as she swam toward the light. She finally made it to land and crawled her way onto the sand.

Once she caught her breath, she looked down at her legs and then at her vagina. Damn, it was fucking beautiful.

Instead of searching for the Prince, she decided to spend a few days alone exploring her sexuality. She found an abandoned boat in a nearby cove and spent the next seventy-two hours eating washed up seaweed and getting to *really* know her vagina. She realized seventeen minutes after discovering a magic button that a vagina was the best thing ever invented.

And if there is one thing in the world worth considering leaving your family for, it's a clitoris.

THE END

SLEEPING BEAUTY GETS WOKE

NCE UPON A TIME...

There lived a radiant and comatose princess named Briar Rose, who lay fast asleep in a castle far, far away. As a baby, Briar Rose had been cursed by the Evil Fairy after her parents forgot to invite the fairy to her Sip & See party. This is a bougie southern kingdom tradition where rich people get drunk on champagne and hang out with a newborn.

Since literally everyone else in the kingdom was invited, the Evil Fairy found out about the bash and decided to crash the soirée. But instead of showing up for the free food and booze, she showed up to curse Briar Rose as revenge for the social snub.

"On her sixteenth birthday, Briar Rose will prick her finger on a spindle and die," she declared while snagging some cheese fondue. After three, maybe four, okay five spoonfuls of gouda, she left in a ball of fire.

Fortunately, another fairy in attendance was able to alter the Evil Fairy's curse.

"Instead of the way-harsh curse of dying," blessed the Good Fairy, "the Princess and the entire castle will fall into a deep sleep and wake when she is kissed by her true love." When confronted about the particulars of her spell many years later, the fairy would claim it wasn't her fault because it had been "a different era."

Fast-forward one hundred years…

The kingdom lay asleep under the Good Fairy's reverse curse. Because of the Good Fairy's blessing, instead of looking like a decrepit centenarian corpse, Briar Rose looked flawless.

A young prince from a neighboring kingdom, who was the captain of his varsity jousting team (a fact he found a way to work into every conversation) heard rumors of this sleeping beauty who could be woken by a kiss. And since locking down a sleeping princess sounded way easier than locking down an awake one, he decided to search for the castle. There began his quest. Road trip!

When he found the hidden castle, he cut through the thorns that had overgrown the palace walls and slayed a dragon, which he couldn't wait to brag about. (However, if he knew anything about dragons, he would have known this one was an extremely small dragon that couldn't even breathe fire.)

The Prince searched every room of the castle until he found the unconscious woman.

"Never have I seen such a dime piece before me," he announced to no one in particular.

He kneeled down close to the Princess.

"I have battled forest vines, an enormous dragon, and a blister on my foot to get to you, Sleeping Beauty. The evil spell shall end, with my kiss upon your super hot lips, which you probably don't understand because curses are too complicated for women to grasp. A curse is a mean spell bad people do," he mansplained. "Also, I brought you these flowers and a six pack."

He began to lean in for a kiss—but before his lips touched hers, a tiny urchin boy cleaning the dungeon floors popped his head in.

"Excuse me, mister," interrupted the boy, adjusting his newsboy cap. "What are you doing?"

The Prince jumped back, startled.

"I'm a prince here to break the spell. The better question is what are you doing? I thought everyone here was asleep."

"They are, except for me. It's my job to get the dust off their spooky dead-but-not-dead bodies. This fairy hired me a couple years ago when the dust had gotten out of control."

"Ah, well, thank you for your hard work. Everyone looks dust-free!"

"Thank you," said the Urchin Boy earnestly.

"Would you like to know my exciting news?" said the Prince. "I'll tell you! There's a way to end the curse and I am here to do it. In fact, only I can break the curse. With a kiss! Also, have I mentioned I'm the captain of my varsity jousting team?"

He expected the Urchin Boy to be rather impressed that he was the one true savior of this kingdom. Instead the Urchin Boy cringed.

"But she's sleeping," said the boy. "You're trying to kiss someone who's sleeping?"

"Okay. After hearing that out loud I understand it might sound a little—"

"—creepy!" interrupted the Urchin Boy. "Very creepy!"

"Look, she pricked her finger, it was a whole thing," said the Prince. "And if I don't kiss her she'll never wake up."

"Let me get this straight," said the boy, setting his mop down and taking a seat between the Prince and Briar Rose. "You're telling me you have to sexually assault a woman to break her from this curse? Because that did not come up in my job interview."

"I'm pretty sure it's not sexual assault if I'm trying to break a curse," said the Prince, gesturing toward the unconscious Princess. "I think if she could talk she'd tell you that she'd want me to kiss her in this situation."

"But you don't know that," said the Urchin Boy. "Because she can't say yes. BECAUSE SHE'S SLEEPING!"

The Prince had come a pretty long way to break this curse and he wasn't about to leave the Princess asleep because some little dude with a mop and a tweed vest was giving him attitude. Plus, she was super hot. Double plus, he hadn't even cracked open his pack of Stud Light yet.

The Prince tossed his cape to the ground.

"It's really hard to be me right now!" he whined. "And it's not supposed to be hard, because I'm a prince."

"Look, mister prince guy, there's really no way around this issue of consent so it's best if you see yourself out."

"My man, why are you trying to lip-block me?"

"I'm not a lip-blocker. I'm a good male ally."

"But I'm her true love," said the Prince.

"But she's never met you," pointed out the Urchin Boy. "So how are you in love?"

This was something that the Prince hadn't considered. He assumed everyone was in love with him. After all, he made the match-winning strike last week at his jousting tournament.

"I mean, I don't think she'd wear that dress if she didn't want me to kiss her," said the Prince, pointing at the Princess's velvety gown.

"Golly gee! That's just what she was wearing when she fell asleep!" said the Urchin Boy, completely appalled. "It's what princesses wear when they hit the balls, because it makes them feel confident and stuff at parties."

"I need a new plan," complained the Prince. "This is an impossible situation and I have been set up for failure."

"Welcome to my entire life as a poor urchin boy," said the boy, staring off into the distance.

But the Prince didn't hear him. He was busy brainstorming and couldn't multitask.

"I have an idea!" the Prince exclaimed. "If you're telling me I shouldn't do a *real* kiss, I'll try a butterfly kiss. Maybe that will work instead."

The Prince leaned in and started fluttering his eyelashes, lightly grazing the Princess's cheek. Nothing happened.

"Damn. I can't believe that didn't work."

"You have to respect her boundaries!" said the Urchin Boy, pushing the Prince away with his mop. "And that was a dumb idea."

But the Prince ignored him.

"Perhaps an eskimo kiss would be better?" he said. He leaned in again, this time rubbing his nose against the nose of her cadaverous body. It didn't work either.

"You're acting like an infected creepy boil!" said the Urchin Boy. "Please stop touching her."

"I've got an idea I think will work this time," said the Prince, brushing him off. "I'll pretend my hand is a mouth."

"No!" said the Urchin Boy. "She needs to agree every time you try something new. And, let me remind you, she hasn't agreed to anything."

But before the Urchin Boy could stop him, the Prince curled his hand into a puppet.

"I'm a mouth, I can talk," he said in a high-pitched puppet voice, flapping his hand. "Have I told you that my varsity jousting team is going to the Realm Championship this year?"

The Urchin Boy sank his head into his palms as the Prince attempted to make out with the Princess using his puppet hand.

"Bummer," said the Prince, when nothing happened.

"You really gotta stop touching her," said the Urchin Boy. "She's unresponsive and it's clearly not working."

"Maybe it didn't work," said the Prince. "But also, she didn't, like, say no."

"Whoa, whoa, whoa," said the Urchin Boy. "Not saying no isn't saying yes. Ever heard of enthusiastic consent? She needs to say yes and she needs to be excited about it. If she wanted you, she'd be grabbing at your fancy tunic."

But the Prince didn't want to go home now. He'd come so far! He had told his whole team he was coming home with a princess. Maybe breaking the curse was like the ten-second rule when you drop your meat pie on the ground: if you pick it up real quick it doesn't count. He'd kiss the Princess real quick, but the kiss wouldn't count. She would never know. It would be like it never happened!

"I'm only doing this to break the curse—no tongue!" he yelled as he went in for a peck on the Princess's mouth before the boy could intervene.

As soon as his lips touched hers, birds began to sing, flowers began to bloom, and everyone in the kingdom raced to the bathroom, because after being asleep for a hundred years they really needed to pee. A glow surrounded the Princess as she opened her eyes and gasped for air. The curse had been lifted! The Prince felt totally vindicated.

"I'm awake!" Briar Rose marveled as she sat up. "Tell me, how was the spell broken, dear strangers?"

Strangers. Shit. The Prince didn't expect her to ask that question.

"Oh, it doesn't really matter," said the Prince, trying to brush it off.

"I must know," urged Briar Rose.

"I'll tell you," said the Urchin Boy, stepping forward as the Prince tried to hold him back. "He stood over you, drooling lustfully, and while you were passed out, he leaned in and kissed you!"

The Princess gasped.

"While I was asleep?!"

She stared at the Prince, while he failed to come up with a reasonable answer to this question.

"You must have been into it since it worked, which means I'm your true love," said the Prince meekly, hoping this would calm her down.

"There's an extremely low threshold for true love in this time period!" screamed the Princess. "Most people are betrothed at birth. If a squirrel kissed me, the curse probably would have been broken, but even a squirrel knows better than to kiss someone who is sleeping and can't give consent!"

This was not how the Prince imagined this situation going down when he left his parents' castle a few days ago to search for her.

"You know what?" said the Prince. "I am so glad you're awake, but, I'm, uh, late for a, uh, sword-polishing hangout with my dad. Anyway. Ta-ta."

And with that, he ran off.

The King and Queen's first proclamation post-wakeup was commanding the Prince to return to their castle to take a sexual harassment and consent workshop.

But the Prince never made it to the workshop. Not because he's entitled and privileged and found a way out of facing even minor consequences for a heinous act, but because on his way to the workshop he got stepped on by a dragon. One that could actually breathe fire.

THE END

SNOW WHITE & THE SEVEN MICROAGGRESSIONS

NCE UPON A TIME...

There lived a vain, evil, and verbally abusive queen, who was the stepmother to a teenager named Snow White. Stepmothers tend to get a bad rap in fairy tales, but this one was truly evil. The Queen was concerned Snow White would one day grow to be more beautiful than herself. Not to psychoanalyze the Evil Queen, but there were clearly some deep-seated issues happening for her to feel so insecure.

Every morning the Evil Queen would look into her Magic Mirror and say:

"Mirror, Mirror, on the wall, who is the fairest of them all?"

And the Magic Mirror would reply, "Beauty is a subjective social construct, the use of the word 'fair' is problematic because it means both 'white' and 'beautiful,' and I terribly hate casting judgment on appearances. But all that aside, you, my Queen, are the fairest of them all."

While the Queen was busy talking to mirrors, Snow White was out living large after moving into a crazy-cute cottage with seven dude roommates who were rarely home. Initially there was a big problem when they left their dishes in the sink and assumed Snow White would deal with the mess. But Snow White put a quick kibosh on that sitch by making a chore chart.

One day, per usual, the Queen asked: "Mirror, Mirror, on the wall, who is the fairest of them all?"

But before answering, the Mirror decided to pay the Evil Queen a compliment.

"You know, I've been meaning to tell you that your use of the gender-neutral pronoun 'them' in your question is quite excellent and inclusive. For an Evil Queen, it's very impressive," said the Mirror.

"Thank you," said the Evil Queen. "Snow White explained to me that they identify as nonbinary and prefer the pronouns 'they' and 'them.' They aren't a maiden, like I thought. So I say 'them' to make sure you include Snow White when I ask who is fairest in the kingdom. Because I'll murder hims, hers, xems, zes, hirs, theys, thems. Really anyone who is hotter than me."

"You are doing an excellent job of respecting Snow White's—"

"Answer my question!" the Evil Queen snapped.

"Like I always say before I answer this question, beauty is a subjective—"

"Blah blah blah, answer the question."

"According to industrialized western white beauty standards, it's no longer you, my Queen. Snow White is the fairest of them all."

"Dammit!" the Evil Queen shouted as she took off her tiara and threw it across the room. "Now I have to kill her."

"Hold up," said the Mirror. "You mean you have to kill *them*. You were doing so well."

"I'm too upset to think about language right now! It's been a huge hassle for me to have to remember every time I'm around her. Them. Whatever!"

"No. It's not whatever. It's really important to Snow White, which is why they had a long conversation with you about it," said the Magic Mirror.

"It's grammatically incorrect anyway."

"Not anymore," explained the Mirror. "Language evolves."

"Okay, fine. I want to kill *them* because *they* are more fair than me. Is that better?"

"In terms of pronouns, yes. In terms of content, absolutely not. Baby steps."

"Great, let's discuss *their* murder."

"Can we focus on one problematic thing at a time?" said the Mirror. "We'll get to why murder is bad later. But since we're on the topic of respectful language, I've been meaning to address something. You see, you have a tendency to commit something called microaggressions on a daily basis. With a lot of people. It's a problem."

"Micro-what?" said the Queen.

"Microaggressions. They are subtle insults made to marginalized people or mirrors. They are typically delivered in everyday interactions by well-intentioned people, so imagine how bad they are delivered by an Evil Queen."

"I do not do that," replied the Evil Queen. "Ask my henchman! Hey, Mark, come over here! Tell the Mirror how nice I am."

The henchman, who lost a leg in a sword fight years ago, came over in his wheelchair.

"You better slow down or you're going to get a speeding ticket in that thing!" said the Queen, laughing.

"That, right there, was a microaggression," said the Magic Mirror. "It's ableism."

"Oh, come on! That's how we joke together," said the Evil Queen. "He likes it."

"Um, actually, your Royal Highness, ma'am, Evil Queen," replied Mark, nervously. "I don't think it's funny. It makes me feel defined by my disability. I've just been too scared of you to say anything. You throw things."

"You're just being lazy," replied the Evil Queen. "You could totally walk and use that peg leg if you wanted to. Also, your shirt is ugly."

There was a long silence in the room. The Magic Mirror blinked at the Evil Queen.

"Okay, fine. I was being mean. But that time it was on purpose. Mark, you are dismissed."

Mark began to head out of the dungeon room. The Evil Queen called after him:

"And bring me Bob, my second henchman. Let's get his opinion on whether I'm doing microaggressions or not. And in the future, you have no reason to be scared of me!"

Mark did as he was told. A few moments later, the Queen's second henchman, Bob, walked in.

"Hi, Bob. Two things. First, I want you to behead Mark. Second, this Mirror thinks I'm committing microaggressions, so I need you to tell it how nice I am."

"Yes, Evil Queen," complied Bob. "You are so nice."

"See, Mirror, I am so nice. Also, can we take a moment to compliment Bob on how great his English is. Where are you from again, Bob?"

"I'm from this kingdom, ma'am," replied Bob.

"No, like, where are you from-from? Originally."

"Okay! That's enough," interrupted the Magic Mirror. "Those were a bunch of microaggressions, back to back! It might seem trivial to you, but when you told Bob his English was good, you implied that he is an outsider in this kingdom, which is a hidden insult. This creates a hostile work environment for Bob. Even more hostile than working for an Evil Queen."

"It was a compliment!" barked the Evil Queen. "Bob doesn't look like he's from here."

"Microaggression alert!" shouted the Mirror.

"That hurts my feelings," said Bob, sheepishly looking at the ground.

"But, Bob, you can admit you're highly sensitive, right? I doubt the other foreign-looking henchman would feel the way you do."

"I don't want to speak for all nonwhite henchmen. I can't possibly represent all of their perspectives. I wouldn't ask you to speak for all Evil Queens."

"Obviously not. I'm special. I'm not like the other ones . . . Okay, I see your point there."

"We're making strides," said the Magic Mirror. "I think you're learning that microaggressions can be unintentional, yet harmful. They are based on institutional oppression and often committed by those in power. And you are very powerful, my Evil Queen."

"Indeed I am! We're done here, Bob. Go behead Mark and then meet me by the guillotine. Don't worry, it's not for you. Well, maybe it is. It will be a surprise! Just meet me there."

Bob nervously walked out the exit.

"Great. Now I have to kill both of my henchmen. Magic Mirror, who am I going to get to kill Snow White and those stupid seven dwarfs? Or, wait, let me guess, 'dwarf' isn't acceptable now?"

"Actually, sometimes it is. The best thing to do is to ask the person what they'd like to be called. Some people with dwarfism prefer 'dwarf' and others prefer 'little people.' They're just people, who don't need to be defined by their size. In general, use their names and if you have to refer to their small stature, saying a 'person with dwarfism' is typically best."

"So I should say, 'Mirror, Mirror, on the wall, how should I kill Snow White and the seven men with dwarfism?'"

"Exactly! In terms of language, at least, you're getting it. At the end of the day, they're just seven adult men who live in a house together. And let's be honest, that's the weird part."

"You know what all this reminds me of? That time I was at the Convention for Evil Leaders and I was the only Evil Queen at the table. The Evil Kings wouldn't listen to me! I had this great idea about how to steal a cyclops and one of the kings pretended it was his idea. So annoying."

"Yes!" exclaimed the Magic Mirror. "Microaggressions are often committed against women, good and evil."

"I ended up having the cyclops behead all of the Evil Kings."

"Of course you did, Your Highness. In the future, let's try to be a little less defensive when someone tells you that you've offended them, be constantly vigilant against your own unconscious biases, and remember that murderous henchmen have feelings, too."

"This has given me a lot to think about. However, don't forget that since Snow White is still the hottest *person* in the kingdom, we still have to kill *them*, as well as the seven men *with dwarfism*, and my hench*people* Mark and Bob, whom I will not define by their disability or racial background."

The Queen smiled proudly. The Magic Mirror beamed back at her.

"We've done great work here today," said the Magic Mirror. "Tomorrow, we'll tackle murder."

THE END

CINDERELLA & THE GLASS CEILING

NCE UPON A TIME...
There lived a strong and resilient young woman named Cinderella, who lived with a mean, demanding, and frankly abusive stepmother and two bratty, dimwitted stepsisters. They spent their time painting bad selfies of themselves that they called "selfie portraits" and they thought almond milk came from cows who ate almonds. Cinderella's mother had tragically died, and her father quickly remarried after just a few dates before you really know who a person is. But soon after, Cinderella's father died, too.

The stepmother resented Cinderella for her empathy in the face of adversity and for being the only one in the family without a widow's peak. She kept the father's money to herself and paid Cinderella minimum wage to become a servant of the house. Cinderella would've loved to be a household manager or one of those well-paid butler types, but those roles always went to the men in the kingdom.

Rent was high in the big city, so the only place Cinderella could afford to live was her stepmother's fireplace, which had a rodent problem and was misleadingly advertised as a cozy studio. On the bright side, the commute was short.

One day, an invitation to a ball hosted by the Royal Prince arrived at the house. The Prince was looking for a bride, and he thought the best way to find one that he hadn't already dated would be to throw a massive party, invite all of the maidens in the kingdom, and then pick one, in what he called a rose ceremony.

Cinderella was ecstatic! "Could marrying the Prince be my way out of poverty? Could I really be royalty? Maybe! Why not?" she mused to her only friends, a bunch of mice.

"Ew, gross, you can't come to the ball with us," said one of her stepsisters, when she found Cinderella in her room sewing a ball gown out of curtains. "People will think you, like, live with us."

"I do live with you," replied Cinderella.

Besides, the invitation clearly read *all maidens*. She'd go to the ball, capture the Prince's heart in her fabulous curtain dress, and finally find out the difference between crudités and raw vegetables.

But before she was supposed to leave for the ball, her stepmother sabotaged her plan. Acknowledging that it was a stepmother's job in fairy tales to be evil and jealous of her stepdaughter, she ripped Cinderella's dress in two and screamed, "I don't have a good reason not to like you, but I just don't! You can't come!" before riding away in a carriage with her two daughters. Cinderella ran outside in tears. Now she didn't have a dress or curtains.

Suddenly, a small, elderly, kind-faced woman appeared in a cloud of silver smoke.

"Mibbidi-mobbidi-moo!" she sang. "It's me, your Fairy Godmother! Dry your tears, Cinderella. You can go to the ball."

And with a swoop of her wand, she turned a pumpkin into a carriage, Cinderella's mice friends into coachmen, and her rags into a beautiful bedazzled ball gown. She also gave her a few more party essentials: breath mints (formerly a piece of lint), décolletage bronzer (formerly birdseed), and red lipstick (formerly pink lipstick).

"Off you go now!" said the Fairy Godmother as she handed Cinderella two glass slippers and disappeared into a flurry of blue bubbles.

"This is my only hope to never clean my stepmother's bidet again," Cinderella told herself as she slipped on the glass shoes. "Let's get this prince to fall in love with me!"

The ball was sensational—with a fountain of champagne, a full orchestra, and a bathroom that had a basket with extra hair ties.

"Would you care to dance?" said a deep voice behind her.

Cinderella turned around. It was the Prince! And while he wasn't as tall as he claimed in his palace bio, she was pleased to see that he was generically handsome. This was the moment she had been waiting for!

"Oh, Cinderella! You're everything I've been looking for!" said the Prince as they spun around the dance floor.

"Tonight is perfect," said Cinderella.

The Prince was moving quickly. Cinderella couldn't believe her luck. She was one step closer to financial security and being famous enough for people to pay you to post sponsored content.

But then she took another step and heard a loud—CRUNCH. She felt a shooting pain in her left foot.

"Oh. My. God," said Cinderella.

She could feel a giant glass shard stabbing her in the arch of her foot. Her glass slipper had shattered.

"What was that?" asked the Prince.

"Oh, nothing," said Cinderella, not wanting to ruin the mood.

CRUNCH. Cinderella took another step. CRUNCH. CRUNCH.

"Okay, I definitely heard that," said the Prince.

"I think my, um, glass slipper might have broken. It's not a big deal. I'm fine! Let's keep dancing," said Cinderella, trying to smile, while she felt the blood pooling in her shoe.

"Hold up. You're wearing slippers … made of glass?" asked the Prince.

"Technically they're glass heels," said Cinderella as she looked around the room at the other women's footwear: satin, sequins, and a few flip-flops on blistered feet.

"Wait a second. Is glass not something the royal gals typically wear?" she asked.

The Prince took a second to assess the situation and quickly realized what the deal was.

"Oh! You must be one of the poor ones we invited," he said.

Cinderella watched the Prince lose interest as he began to scan the room, looking for other maidens to dance with.

"Wait! It's not that bad. I can still dance—look!" Cinderella said as she did a little twirl for the Prince, limping terribly. "I've heard that heels are painful. This is probably what people mean."

CRUNCH.

"Owww—ahhh—Iiiiiiii love dancing so much!" Cinderella yelled, trying to cover the crackle of glass. Judging from the look on the Prince's face, it wasn't working.

"Let's take a break," said the Prince, slowly walking backward.

"No, please!" said Cinderella, pulling him toward her. "I'm having a great time. I thought the mini-quiche was incredible. I ate it in one bite."

"That's disgusting," scoffed the Prince. "Everyone knows about the four-bite rule. A mini quiche should take you a good ninety minutes to finish."

So that's why no one at this ball has food in their mouth when they talk, thought Cinderella. Who were these snobby gate-keepers coming up with etiquette that made it impossible for her to effortlessly fit in?

Cinderella tried to go back to dancing, but without moving her feet. She looked like one of those inflatable dancing tube men outside of carriage dealerships.

"I don't want a little broken glass to ruin this date," said Cinderella. "It's really important. If you don't fall in love with me, I'm gonna be dusting floorboards for the rest of my life."

"I mean, that's not really on me," said the Prince.

Wow. The Prince was being a real dungeon-bag. But he was also an easy way out of Cinderella's dreadful living situation. Her mind raced: should she try to make it work with this guy or should she tell him off and spit in his champagne? Convincing herself that maybe he was just hangry since it takes rich people so long to eat their food, she decided on the former.

"I actually didn't buy these glass slippers myself," explained Cinderella. "They were a gift and it seemed rude not to wear them."

"When I think a gift is ugly I just throw it away," said the Prince.

"They were my only option," said Cinderella. "I don't own a pair of shoes."

"Not even boat shoes?" asked the Prince. "Or those ones with the red bottoms that ladies love?"

"I sleep in a fireplace," she quipped. "How would I know anything about gender-normative footwear?"

"Whoa, whoa, whoa. You sleep in a fireplace?"

"Yeah, that's why my name is Cinder ... ella."

"I thought it was just a trendy name, like Brooklyn," said the Prince.

Cinderella began to tear up, but not because this reminded her how she could never find her name on one of those souvenir keychains. She realized she had been pretending to be someone she wasn't to win over this loser because he was in a better socioeconomic position than her. She deserved love just the way she was—without a designer ball gown or a sweet carriage. Also, her foot really freaking hurt.

"Can someone get this woman a mop so she can clean up all this foot blood?" the Prince shouted into the air.

"Where is my Fairy Godmother when I need her?" Cinderella cried. "I gotta get out of here."

"You have a Fairy Godmother?" asked the Prince, disgusted. "Wow, you're poorer than I thought. Everyone in this room has an inheritance."

Suddenly her Fairy Godmother appeared in a poof of purple glitter.

"Fibbidi-fobbidi—oh, dear godmother!" she shrieked when she saw the blood spilling out from Cinderella's shoe. "What happened to your foot?"

"The glass slippers," replied Cinderella, unamused.

"You put those on your feet?" asked the Fairy Godmother. "I guess I should have been more clear. Those are paperweights."

"They're what?" asked Cinderella, baffled.

"You were supposed to give them to the King and Queen as a castlewarming gift," explained the Fairy Godmother. "If they were shoes, I would have put them on your feet myself. I specifically remember handing them to you."

"I'm a servant!" cried Cinderella. "How am I supposed to know rich people like paperweights in the shape of shoes?"

"My bad," said the Fairy Godmother.

The Prince picked up the unbroken right shoe and placed it on his head.

"Maybe it's a hat!" he said, laughing. "What do you think of my glass hat?"

Everyone in the ballroom laughed at the Prince's joke. It was the hardest they'd laughed since the time he made a joke about a priest, a rabbi, and a minotaur walking into a tavern.

Cinderella wasn't sure if it was watching the Prince make fun of her or if it was the lack of blood in her body, but she began to get light-headed.

"You know what?" she screamed. "Maybe I was stupid to put the glass slippers on my feet, but don't tell me any of the heels in this room are any more comfortable! Are they? Are they?"

"They're not!" shouted a nearby brunette waving one of her flip-flops in the air.

The Prince and Fairy Godmother looked for an escape but noticed the rest of the room had gone silent, watching.

"I'll say it. I was trying to win the royal lottery by coming tonight, hoping I could easily move up social classes by becoming one of you," Cinderella continued. "That's a false idea that is perpetuated in society as a possibility but almost never happens because the system is broken. What I'd actually need to do to get out of poverty is nearly impossible, because you rich people have set up the world in your favor. And I'm not talking party favors. Although I've seen the gift bag and it's exceptional."

People slowly started approaching the gift bag table while she continued to talk.

"I'm in this situation because the world has set me up to fail. For me to get an education and achieve financial stability, I need to pray I get some sort of grant or scholarship or magic beans. And if I am lucky enough to receive help, I'll still need to work two jobs on the side to barely get by. I'll be buried in student loans, living paycheck to paycheck with no one to fall back on or help me. Any setback could mean failure: medical bills, losing a job, or getting cursed by an evil witch."

Everyone in the castle stared at the Prince, waiting for his response.

"Look, Cindy," muttered the Prince. "I'd hire you here at the castle, but the only job openings are for royal advisers. You know, important, high-level stuff. That a woman can't do."

"This is what I'm talking about!" said Cinderella. "On top of everything I've just said, I'm also being held back because I'm a woman. But guess what? You see how I broke this glass slipper? Watch how I break the glass ceiling!"

Everyone in the room ducked for cover and peered nervously at the glass dome above the ballroom.

"Not the actual glass ceiling, you idiots! I'm talking about the metaphorical glass ceiling that represents the invisible barrier holding back women and people of color from advancing professionally … I can't believe you're all opening your gift bags while I'm giving this speech."

Cinderella hobbled out of the room, looking back one last time.

"I'll go to school, I'll get a job, rise the ranks, and call myself Chief Glass Disrupter on my business card because I'll work at one of those cool companies where you make up your own title. You'll see. All of you!" said Cinderella. "Oh, and by the way, 'crudités' is just a fancy word for regular vegetables."

Cinderella left that night and did everything she said she would do. It wasn't easy, of course, but Cinderella persisted. She shattered the glass ceiling into as many pieces as she had shattered that stupid glass paperweight.

And she always wore flats.

THE END

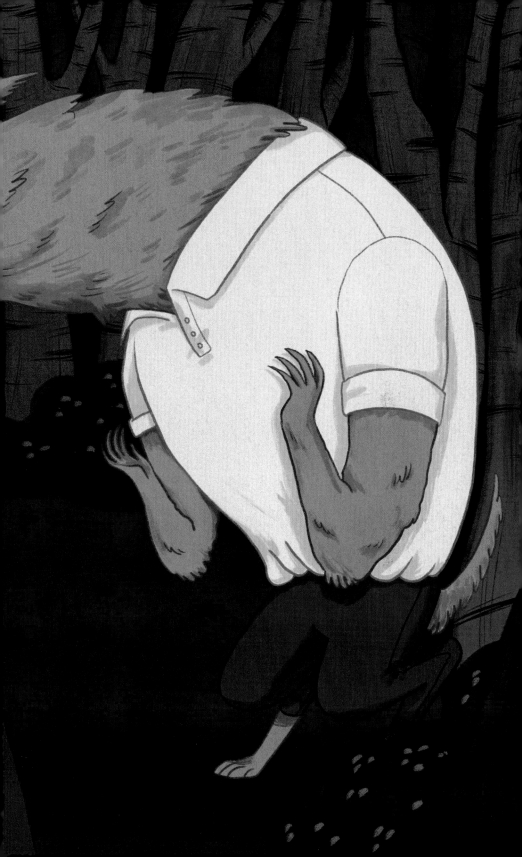

LITTLE RED RIDING HOOD &
THE BIG BAD WOLFCALLER

NCE UPON A TIME...

There lived a considerate and spirited young woman named Little Red Riding Hood. Actually her name was Rosa. But because she wore a cherry-colored cape and was 5'2" everyone in town called her Little Red Riding Hood. They were extremely uncreative with nicknames.

One day, Rosa's mother asked her to take her abuela a basket of pan dulce because she was sick.

"Be sure you go straight to Abuela's," said her madre. "Don't walk down dark streets, don't talk to strangers, and don't slouch, mija."

"I got it, Ma!" Rosa responded as she headed out the door and immediately slouched her shoulders again.

After walking a few blocks toward Abuela's, Rosa heard a loud, long whistle from behind a tree.

"Arh-wooooooooooooooo!"

It was a wolf!

"Hey there, Red. Nice cape," said the wolf. "Bet you look even better without it."

Ugh, what a pain, Rosa thought to herself. She was not in the mood to deal with an unwanted wolfcaller. Not that any wolfcallers were wanted. Also, what an unoriginal wolfcall. I mean, come on! It was just bold outerwear!

Rosa took out a chocolate cookie from the basket and began to nibble as a distraction.

"That cookie looks muy sabrosa," said the wolf, smiling creepily at Rosa. "May I have a bite?"

Who asks strangers for a bite of their dessert? thought Rosa. *Leave me alone.*

She considered throwing the half-eaten cookie at him, but it was too good to waste on a wolf. She quickened her pace instead.

But the wolf continued to follow her as she raced over a footbridge.

"Mmmmhmmmm," crooned the wolf in a disturbing tone. "Tasty."

She hoped the wolf was referring to the food and not her. She scanned the area, looking to see if there was a safe space to go inside and hide, but the stores were closed and even the food carriages were empty.

The wolf was still following her and Rosa was getting more and more uncomfortable. She didn't want to have a confrontation with the wolf and anger him, but perhaps eye contact—or better yet, a demeaning eye roll—would make him stop. She looked directly in his yellow eyes and said, "Ich," as she threw her head back in an exaggerated eye roll.

"Damn, that ass," said the wolf.

Whelp, that didn't work, thought Rosa. She lowered her head and pulled on the hood of her red cape, hoping he would get the hint and stop.

"Smile, honey. Why won't you give me a smile?" asked the wolf as he got closer. "What's your problem, bitch?"

Now his wolfcalls were getting aggressive. Ignoring him wasn't working, acknowledging him wasn't working, and Rosa was desperate to do something to make him stop. Her palms got sweaty, she felt the blood rise to her cheeks, and her left eye got twitchy. She would try one last tactic: the impassioned monologue.

"Hey, wolf. You're making me uncomfortable," said Rosa. "I am trying to visit my sick abuela. I would like to be able to walk down a public street without getting harassed about my food, my cloak, or my ass, which by the way you can't even see because it's entirely covered by my cape! We are both creatures on this planet, just trying to go about their day. How would it feel if I reduced you to your excessively furry gray tail? I don't like when you talk to me like that. It doesn't make me feel good. It makes me feel bad. I didn't pick this cloak for you. I picked it for me. And for my mom, because this is the only item of clothing she agrees is cute. In the future, please try to talk to women in a more respectful tone. Que tengas un buen día. Adios."

The wolf stopped in his tracks. Rosa didn't wait to see what he would do. She turned around and hustled toward Abuela's house.

She questioned whether she should have said anything to him at all. What if he had a weapon or really sharp teeth? Sometimes wolfcallers were dangerous and, in some cases, they had rabies.

When she finally peeked behind her shoulder, the wolf was gone. *Wow! Guess monologues work after all,* she thought.

However, just to be safe, she did what any young woman does when they feel uncomfortable: she sent a location pigeon to her best friend Cleo to tell her where she was. Location pigeons were great when you were meeting up with friends to see a concert in the forest or when you were being stalked by a canine.

Soon Rosa had arrived at Abuela's.

She knocked on the door and waited, but Abuela didn't answer. Rosa tried the door, and to her surprise, it was unlocked.

"Hola, Abuela! It's Rosa!" she yelled. "I brought you treats and snacks."

"In here, mija," said Abuela. But it didn't sound like Abuela at all. Her voice sounded raspy and ragged, like a pipe-a-day ogre. *Poor Abuela*, thought Rosa, *she must be really sick.*

Rosa reached Abuela's room at the back of the house and pushed open the door. There was her Abuela, curled up in bed reading a book. But something looked off.

"My, what big ears you have, Abuela," said Rosa.

"All the better to hear you with."

"My, what big eyes you have."

"All the better to see you with."

"My, what a big mouth you have."

"Okay, that's enough!" said her abuela. "It's not very nice of you to comment on my big eyes, ears, and mouth. Ear cartilage stretches with age, my new reading glasses magnify my eyes, and I got new dentures."

"Sorry," said Rosa. "I barely recognized you with those new glasses. They look great!"

"So tell me, how was your walk, mija?"

"To be honest, not so good," said Rosa as she climbed into bed with her sage and all-knowing abuela. "There was this wolf-caller who was following me and he wouldn't leave me alone."

Rosa explained what happened on the walk over.

"You know," said Abuela, "at my age, I still get wolfcalled, too."

Rosa didn't find this too surprising. After all, women of all ages, shapes, and sizes get wolfcalled.

"I wish I had wise words for you, but the fact is, even among my abuela amigas, there's no true consensus on how to deal with wolfcallers. All of my amigas have different strategies. At the end of the day, it's situational. If you don't do anything, it doesn't feel very empowering, but if you fight back, there's the risk of danger. I'm proud of how you handled that piece of troll garbage and sad excuse for a wolf. Now, may I have one of your mother's delicious pan dulce?"

They spent the next hour eating sweets and fantasizing about how they wished they could respond to wolfcallers. Abuela wished she could smack them across the face, while Rosa dreamed of presenting a scroll slideshow on why wolfcalling makes women feel unsafe.

"I'm really glad you're okay," said Rosa to Abuela. "I had this strange fear the wolf was a home-invading serial killer who would follow me back here and eat you, and then try to eat me."

"Well, it's just me," said Abuela. "Maybe that's a different wolf, in a different, even darker, stranger tale."

Meanwhile, across town, the wolf was still wolfcalling other women who were out for a stroll. That is, until his own grandma spotted him while she was out getting bread. As he made kissing sounds and screamed at a young woman: "Baby, I'd hit that—" his grandma stuck out her giant sourdough loaf and tripped him. As he lay on the sidewalk, she lectured her grandwolfson on male aggression and toxic masculinity.

And he never wolfcalled again.

THE END

RAPUNZEL'S ARMPITS

NCE UPON A TIME...

There lived an independent and fearless young woman in a tall tower with only one way up and one way down: by climbing her long silky locks of hair. As a baby, she had been taken from her parents by a witch after her father was caught stealing vegetables from the witch's garden for his then-pregnant wife. The witch believed this had been a classic case of toxic masculinity—a man thinking he could take whatever he wanted without asking.

The witch named the baby after one of the stolen vegetables, rapunzel. This may sound like a weird name but it was way better than her other choice, broccolini. Wanting to keep Rapunzel as protected from a male-dominated society as possible, the witch locked her in a tower with no way to escape. She had Rapunzel grow her hair as long as the tower, so when the witch wanted to do some light parenting, Rapunzel would throw down her hair, and the witch would climb up.

Climbing hair served two purposes. It taught Rapunzel to screw beauty standards by using her long locks for utilitarian purposes. And it was way easier than moving a ladder back and forth.

"All men want your vegetables," the witch said to Rapunzel before putting her to sleep each night.

One day, many years later, a man on a horse rode by and watched the witch climb the luxurious hair of the most beautiful woman he'd ever seen. And—you guessed it—he was a prince.

Once the witch had left and the coast was clear, he approached Rapunzel's tower and called up to her as the witch had:

"Rapunzel! Rapunzel! Let down your hair, so that I may climb thy flowing stair."

Rapunzel stuck her head out of the tower window and looked down.

"A prince!" she said. "How did thee find me?"

"From a distance, I saw a woman climb thy silky tresses that shine like the stars," called the Prince. "May I come up?"

"Are your intentions honorable and your heart gold?" asked Rapunzel.

"Yes, my lady. Oh, how I have longed to meet a beauty such as thee!"

"And by beauty, do you mean the feminine beauty ideal based on heteronormative assumptions that was created to keep women down? Not down from towers, but you know what I mean."

"Oh, um, of course not. I definitely meant … inner beauty?" said the Prince. "Inner beauty is still okay, right?"

"Indeed it is! I shall let down my hair."

The Prince was ecstatic as he watched Rapunzel lean back to launch down her locks.

"I can't wait to get my hands on those soft, silky—holy crap," said the Prince as he watched Rapunzel toss down a bundle of long, dark, sweaty hair.

"Oh my god," he said to himself. "That is not head hair. That's armpit hair."

The Prince hesitated, unsure of what to do. Because while it's not normal to climb someone's head hair, it is unheard of to climb someone's armpit hair. The Prince hadn't been this grossed out since a bunch of knights pranked him a few years back by Dutch-ovening his suit of armor.

Sure, he considered himself a feminist, but he still didn't want to climb armpit hair. He just wasn't into it. He stared at the pile of coarse hair next to him.

"Is there a problem?" Rapunzel yelled down.

"It's, um, armpit hair," replied the Prince. "A little weird, no?"

"Weird?" said Rapunzel. "You don't think it's weird I grow out my head hair 165 feet but you think it's weird I grow out my armpit hair?"

"I guess both are weird."

"Wrong answer. I can do whatever I want to my body."

"Right, right, right!" he replied, realizing he had made a mistake. "I didn't mean bad weird! I just meant I was expecting to climb your head hair, like that crazy witch did."

"Whoa. That crazy witch is my mom," said Rapunzel.

"Crap. Sorry!" replied the Prince, fumbling. "Let me start over. I was expecting to climb your head hair, like your mother, who wears all black clothes and a pointy black hat."

"My head is sore," said Rapunzel. "Also, I think it looks cool. Women in other kingdoms grow out their armpit hair all the time."

The Prince could tell things were not going smoothly. He needed to step up his game if he was going to have a chance with Rapunzel.

"You're right, I'm coming up!" he said as he took a deep breath. "This is something I am doing."

He took hold of her armpit hair and began to climb.

"I love women," he yelled up. "I am against patriarchal views of how a woman should look or how they should wear their hair. I always say, women should get swords!"

The Prince had never before expressed an opinion on women getting weaponry.

The climb was rather long but the view was fantastic. However, halfway up the Prince started to sniff something strange.

"What's the problem now?" asked Rapunzel.

"Nothing," said the Prince.

"Your mouth is saying one thing but your face is saying another," she replied.

"It sorta smells," he admitted, too overwhelmed by the stench to come up with a kinder response.

"I use organic nontoxic deodorant. The other kind gives you cancer," Rapunzel retorted, clearly annoyed. "I've had enough of corporations run by lords hawking beauty products to ladies that are pumped full of toxic chemicals detrimental to our health."

"Yes, yes, that is the worst," stammered the Prince, realizing he was getting deeper and deeper into the dragon house. "I always say, Lords, keep your sulfates to yourself."

He'd never said that before in his life.

As the Prince got closer to Rapunzel's balcony, he noticed she was wearing bright red lipstick and a set of lashes.

"Oh," said the Prince as he climbed. "I wouldn't have expected someone like you to be wearing makeup."

"Someone like *me*?" said Rapunzel.

Uh, oh, thought the Prince. *I think I've done something wrong again, but I'm not sure what.*

"I can do whatever makes me feel good," said Rapunzel. "Feminists can wear falsies."

"Yes. I always say that!" said the Prince. "Feminists can wear falsies." The Prince had no idea what a falsie was.

Finally, the prince climbed into Rapunzel's tower. *Thank goodness,* he thought, *I don't want to talk about beauty standards anymore. It's too complicated.*

"Rapunzel! What a lovely turret you have," he said. "Now if you want to come check out my palace later, we could tie your sheets together, bust you out of here and I could give you a ride back on my horse. But I'm not sure there's room for, like, all of your body hair."

He took another look at her armpit hair that wrapped around the room.

"Definitely just your head hair," he said. "But don't worry, I have a sword you can use to shave."

Rapunzel rolled her eyes.

"I'm good," she said flatly. "You don't get it. You need to leave. Boy, bye."

"What?" said the Prince, confused. "I spent forty-five minutes climbing your armpit hair and now I have to leave? I thought we were hitting it off!"

"Newsflash: nobody wants someone to tell them how to look," said Rapunzel. "The beauty ideal is deeply internalized. Maidens get bombarded with mixed messages about appearance every day. We're told we are superficial for wanting to self-express through beauty and makeup while at the same time we get judged if we fail to live up to the unattainable standard of femininity. Apparently, there's no escaping the noble male gaze. Even when you live in a tower. Time for you to go!"

"Wait—before I climb your armpits again, what about leg hair? Is that an option?" asked the Prince, desperately.

"No. I shave my legs."

"After all of this, you shave your legs?" he said.

"If there is one thing you should have learned today, it's that it's my choice," said Rapunzel. "And judging me for it makes you a part of the problem."

The Prince began to think about his role in the "noble male gaze" and perpetuating the patriarchy, but then he remembered he was hungry and cared about that more.

"Do you know where they serve a good veggie stew around here?"

"All you men want is our damn vegetables!" shouted Rapunzel as she reached under her gown and tossed down her tower-length pubic hair.

Surprise!

"Climb my bush," said Rapunzel. "My armpits are sore now."

And with that, the Prince climbed down Rapunzel's gloriously long pubes and never returned.

THE END

MULAN'S MOOLA

NCE UPON A TIME...

There lived a courageous and persistent woman named Mulan. At eighteen years old she enlisted in the Chinese Army and disguised herself as a man to fight in place of her aging father. She fought for twelve years without her fellow warriors ever discovering her secret. Mulan mastered the art of upright urination thanks to her invention of the original female funnel.

When Mulan decided to retire after the war, she finally told everyone the truth: she was a woman and their dick jokes weren't funny. The army was shocked that this decorated war hero was a "chick." Who knew women could fight just as well as men and look good with short hair? After Mulan's announcement, the Chinese army decided to let women enlist. Mulan retired in peace, knowing she'd never have to go near a urinal again.

But did you know Mulan's story continued?

Mulan moved back to her hometown, got married, and had a son. Five years later, she heard a knock at the door. It was her old army boss, General Li.

"Mulan, we're at war again," General Li said. "We need you back! I'm offering you a promotion to be one of the lieutenant generals training our warriors. And I've doubled the budget for Dim Sum Fridays! You'll accept, right?"

She had been considering going back to work recently, and also, she missed the commissary soup dumplings. "I'm in!" said Mulan.

Two months into training, Mulan's troops were weeks ahead of the other units. They were stronger, faster, and were the only troops who could Hula-Hoop for forty-five minutes straight. The last part doesn't sound like it's a skill that would help out in war, but hip flexibility is very underrated.

One day during lunch at the mess hall, Mulan started making small talk with another lieutenant general.

"This Peking duck is delicious," said Mulan as she plopped a bite in her mouth. "What Chef Zhang can do with canned wartime food is insane."

"Don't tell the chef, but I swiped a little extra," said Lieutenant General Wu.

"I won't tattle, but you gotta share," she said, smiling.

As he passed her a piece of his food, a paper fell out of his coat pocket and landed at Mulan's feet. She reached down to pick it up. It was his paycheck. And he was making some serious dough.

"Did you ask for an advance or are you on some different pay schedule?" she asked, puzzled.

"No, that's just my weekly rate," he said, before realizing something was wrong. "Don't we all make this?"

Nope. What Mulan made in a month, Lieutenant General Wu made in a week. Mulan was shocked. And frankly, she was embarrassed. After all, they had the same job, the same rank, and the same Chinese zodiac sign (the Rooster: ambitious but with no patience for crossword puzzles).

She had assumed there was a standard rate for the position so she hadn't thought to bring it up. Also, it felt rude to discuss money with other warrior killing machines.

But politeness hadn't done her coin pouch any favors. She realized battling for your pay was no different than battling for your country: the opponent doesn't give you anything unless you fight for it. She would go to General Li first thing in the morning. Mulan wanted her moola.

The next day, she put on her favorite suit of armor and backed up her list of spies, just in case things went south and she needed to quit on the spot.

She knocked on General Li's tent.

"We need to discuss my pay," Mulan said to General Li when he opened the flap. "I'm making way less yuan than the male lieutenant generals. During the last war, I made the same as my peers."

"The budget had tightened by the time you were hired. We are at war, after all," said General Li. "Also, back then I thought you were a dude."

"What?!"

"I'm sorry, Mulan. It's not gonna happen. Come back in a few months and we'll talk."

But Mulan was prepared to defend her position. She had brought all the ammunition she needed: a bunch of spreadsheets full of cold hard data.

"My troops are six weeks ahead of every other unit, which means I'm saving the army 200,000 yuan a week. I oversee 30,000 warriors, as many as the other lieutenant generals. Plus,

I've convinced them to go commando which is saving a ton of money on laundry."

"That sounds really uncomfortable."

"It's a little cold but they got used to it," said Mulan.

"Look, your husband also works so your paycheck is secondary income. And your coworkers didn't take time off to have a child, so…"

"Whoa! That motherhood penalty crap should not be held against me," said Mulan. "Also, having a child didn't diminish my skill set. If anything it helped! Changing a little boy's diaper is really all about hand-eye coordination."

Before he could say anything, Mulan decided to go in for the kill. Old rules said to wait for your boss to give a salary number first, but Mulan knew that could lead to getting lowballed.

"I'm a proven war hero who has mastered martial arts, sword fighting, and fishtail braids. I want 700,000 yuan a year, like the other guys, plus back pay with interest," she said firmly. "And I need a chariot that doesn't squeak."

"Mulan, you know I'm on your side," said General Li. "But unfortunately it's out of my hands. It really comes down to budget. You aren't going to make us choose between your salary and armor for your troops, right? Do you want to have that over your head?"

Mulan was furious—she knew a man wouldn't be guilt-tripped like this. Men who asked to get paid more were seen as ambitious, while women were viewed as materialistic. Mulan didn't have time for this double standard.

She thought about the reasons to stay at the job: it wasn't like she could join some other army, and also her troops had planned a fun flash mob for lunch tomorrow.

But on the other hand, this was dragon dung.

"I understand—" said Mulan.

"I thought you would," replied General Li.

"*I understand* that I am worth what I've asked you for. I'm putting in my resignation today. Thank you for your time."

And with that, she packed up her sword, suits of armor, and secret candy stash and went home.

This wasn't about her. Most women didn't have the option of quitting their job to stand up for what they believed in, because they had bills to pay. This was for them and for future generations of women and women pretending to be men.

The army went to war without Mulan's courage, leadership, and Hula-Hooping prowess, and after a few battles, they were losing badly and their hips were stiff. After one particularly devastating fight, Mulan got another knock at the door. It was General Li, sheepishly shuffling his feet.

"Listen, we need you back. And this time I'll pay you what you asked for. Also, have I mentioned I've added green tea on tap in the mess hall?"

"I don't drink caffeine," said Mulan, stone-faced.

"I also moved the entire army to equal pay."

"Now that's something I drink. It's about time!"

Mulan returned to the army and helped China defeat the enemy while riding her brand-new nonsqueaky chariot.

At the end of the war, Mulan sat down with General Li.

"Amazing job!" he exclaimed. "You really are worth every penny. And can you believe we won both wars? China's War and the Equal Pay War!"

"Oh no, honey, we haven't even started the second war."

"Come again?"

"There's the larger issue of the gender pay gap," said Mulan. "Even with equal pay, if women are being held back from promotions, they'll still make significantly less than men overall. I'm the only female lieutenant general in the army, which is great for mirror space in the bathroom, but not great for equality."

Mulan went on to fight the hardest battle she'd ever fought: the systemic problems behind the gender pay gap. She rode throughout the country helping women negotiate their salaries, encouraging young women to enter higher-paying careers, tearing down the barriers to education, fixing the lack of paid family leave, and teaching everyone how to do a fishtail braid.

The Battle for Mulan's Moola had just begun ...

THE END

NEVER, NEVER MAN

ONCE UPON A TIME...

There lived the Darling family and their three children: Wendy, John, and the youngest and most photographed, Michael. The three children shared a nursery together where they would read stories, play checkers, and practice sewing, because that's what kids did before they stared at screens.

One night after one of Wendy's stories, she relayed some bad news to her siblings.

"John, Michael, tonight is my last night in the nursery. I won't be able to tell any more stories," she said. "Mom and Dad say I have to grow up. I get my own room, which sounds really cool except this means I'm one step closer to having to do my own taxes."

Just then, a boy in green clothing and a strange pointy hat with a feather flew into the nursery and announced: "No more stories? I don't think so! You'll come with me to Neverland, where you'll never grow up! Oh, and by the way, I'm Peter Pan."

"So fun! I'll grab our passports," said Wendy, who for some reason didn't think it was at all bizarre for a boy she had never met to fly in through the window.

Suddenly, a tiny fairy burst into the nursery, also in green clothing and with a perfectly messy topknot that looked casual but took a good twenty minutes to do. She flew around the room, circling above the Darlings' heads while making a loud bell noise.

Ding, ding, ding!

"What is that shrill bell?" asked Wendy.

"Oh, that's Tinker Bell. You can't understand what she's saying, because she speaks Neverland language, like I do," explained Peter Pan. "But don't worry, I can translate."

"Wonderful!" said Wendy. "I want to know what she's saying."

"I hope she can vouch for this stranger who has come into our nursery," said John, but no one listened to him, because everyone ignores the middle child.

Little Michael nodded. He couldn't talk yet.

Ding, ding, ding!

"Kids, do not come!" said Tinker Bell, in her Neverland language, which sounded like if every doorbell in your neighborhood went off at the same time. "This guy is a creep. He's been sitting in your window at night, listening to your stories and staring at you. For months."

The children looked up at Peter Pan, waiting for him to translate.

"Um, yeah, so … she says you should come to Neverland and you will love it," Peter lied.

Ding, ding, ding!

"Peter, that's not what I said!" said Tink, flying madly around the children's heads. "Wendy, you are not the first girl he's brought to Neverland. The others haven't come back. Ever wonder what happened to that girl Seraphina who lived down the street? She didn't move away. She got captured by a pirate and then got eaten by a crocodile!"

But the children couldn't understand her. All they heard were bells.

"She can't wait for you to meet the friendly crocodile," said Peter Pan.

"What she said was a lot longer," said John, but no one heard him, because he was born three years after Wendy and six years before Michael.

"What she said was a lot longer," said Wendy.

Tinker Bell breathed a sigh of relief. They were starting to catch on.

"Neverland language is long. That's why it can never be subtitled in movies. *'Ding ding ding ding ding ding ding ding ding ding ding ding ding ding ding ding ding ding ding'* means 'bread.' Linguistics, am I right?" said Peter. "Anyway, you'll come with me to Neverland and never come back home again!"

Ding, ding, ding!

"Girl, he's not lying about the last part," said Tink. "If he says, 'Second star from the right and straight on 'til morning' get out of there. That's his line. And it's not even a good one."

Tinker Bell pulled at Peter Pan's clothes, trying to usher him toward the window to leave.

Ding, ding, ding!

"Time to go, buddy," she said.

"Why is she trying to get you to leave?" asked John. But nobody heard him, because he was born neither first nor third in the succession of the Darling children.

"Why is she trying to get you to leave?" asked Wendy.

"Okay, I really didn't want to make this awkward, but I suppose I should just be honest with you. I didn't tell her there'd be another girl here," said Peter. "And you know how needy women can get."

Ding, ding, ding!

"Needy?" cried Tinker Bell. "You're the one who needs my dust to fly! And for the record, you said you were going bowling."

She flew around in circles and began to tear up.

"She is so emotional and hormonal," said Peter to the children as he led them toward the window.

Ding, ding, ding!

"Emotional?" cried Tinker Bell. "Yes, I am emotional! Wanna know why? I am trying to stop you from kidnapping these children."

Tinker Bell pulled at Wendy's hair, trying to steer them back toward the center of the room and away from the window. Pulling hair is typically done by playground bullies, unless you're a small fairy trying to save a young girl and her siblings from being abducted by a dude in tights.

"Ow! Ow! Ow!" cried Wendy. "She's pulling my hair!"

"Now she's telling me she's jealous of you, because you're her competition," said Peter Pan. "She thinks you're trying to steal her man. That's me. I'm a man. Sorta."

Ding, ding, ding!

Tinker Bell looked deep into Wendy's eyes hoping she would understand.

"Wendy, he's trying to pit us against each other," said Tinker Bell. "Women have been conditioned to believe that other women are out to get them. We're told there is only one slot for a woman at the top and you need to compete against other women to claim it. But that isn't true. Girl, I'm trying to help you!"

"She says your nightgown makes you look fat," said Peter.

Wendy gasped. Peter Pan yanked Tinker Bell over to the side of the nursery, out of the children's earshot.

"You need to chill. I'm 1,400 years old. I can do whatever the fuck I want! And what I want is to bring these kids to Neverland. Get with the program!"

Tears streamed down Tinker Bell's face. She didn't think there was any way she could convince the Darling children not to come to Neverland. They'd soon be stuck in a place with vicious reptiles, racist portrayals of Native Americans, and a poor excuse for sleeping arrangements.

The children's eyes tick-tocked back and forth between the distressed fairy and the irate man-child screaming at her. This was not the look of a jealous girl. This was the look of someone who had your back.

"I think he's lying," said John.

"I think he's lying," whispered tiny Michael, speaking for the first time in his life.

"You can talk!" said Wendy. "Also, I think you're right, Michael."

"Oh, come on! That was a whisper. Why can't anyone hear me?" said John.

Wendy looked at Tinker Bell and noticed she was motioning toward the window. The fairy had a plan and Wendy understood exactly what it was. Wendy locked eyes with Tinker Bell, saying silently, "I got you." Tinker Bell nodded back.

"Follow Tink's lead," Wendy whispered to her siblings before walking over to Peter Pan.

"Peter, do we have to bring her with us?" said Wendy coyly. "Couldn't we perhaps leave her behind?"

Peter's eyes lit up.

"Wendy, you're right!" said Peter, giving Tinker Bell a cruel glare. "We can leave her here."

Peter took Wendy's hand and led her toward their fourth-floor window.

"Come on, Wendy, off we go!" said Peter triumphantly. "Second star to the right and straight on 'til morning. We're off to Neverlaaaaaaaand!"

But before they jumped into the sky, Wendy let go of his hand. They both teetered on the window sill. Wendy's siblings and Tinker Bell yanked her nightgown and pulled her back inside the room. Peter windmilled his arms ready to fly, but with no dust, gravity took hold.

"You forgot about my fairy dust!" yelled Tinker Bell as Peter Pan fell four stories below. His skull smashed against the cobblestones and bits of his brains and blood splattered on the Darling family's front stoop.

The two brothers looked down, horrified.

"Well, boys. That's why you shouldn't lie to women," said Wendy. "And why I keep telling Mom and Dad we need child-safety window guards."

THE END

BEAUTY AND THE BEAST & THE OTHER KIDNAPPED WOMEN YOU HAVEN'T HEARD ABOUT

NCE UPON A TIME...

There lived a confident and bright young white woman named Belle. She lived in a small town in the French countryside with her kind, directionally challenged, and balding father. In fairy tales, bald guys are either evil villains or loveable doofuses. Belle's dad was the latter. Belle was loved by the town for both her friendliness (she said "Bonjour!" to everyone) and her smarts (she was the only one in town who could read a clock).

One day her father got lost in the woods. He found himself on the grounds of a castle owned by a beast and was taken prisoner for trespassing.

Who was this luxury property–owning beast? Well, years ago, an enchantress decided to test a prince's character by disguising herself as a beggar and asking to stay the night in his castle during a storm. The Prince refused, and as punishment the enchantress turned him into a beast, making his exterior look like his interior: ghastly and grisly, with ingrown toenails.

Another part of the curse was that all of his staff was turned into animated household objects. Because if there's one thing selfish rich men in power are good at, it's sinking the whole ship with them.

When Belle's father didn't return, she searched for him, found the castle, and became prisoner in exchange for her father. A popular buff bro in town tried to rescue her, but she rejected him and decided to live with the beast instead because she wasn't into butt chins. We know this is complicated, but stories from the 1700s are very plot-heavy.

But did you know there's a part of the fairy tale you haven't heard? You see, this wasn't the only prince this happened to. The enchantress tested multiple princes in the kingdom and those who didn't let her stay the night were also cursed. Soon there were many castles run by beasts, full of talking furniture. Apparently entitled asshole princes were a systemic problem in the kingdom.

And here's the thing about beasts: they have pretty kidnappy vibes. The beasts captured anyone who stumbled on their grounds, which meant any woman out for an adventure, a nice jog, or a new place to get a brew.

There were a lot of women being abducted, but you've probably only heard of one: that pretty white woman named Belle. So we're going to tell a tale about one of the other missing women. The reason you haven't heard this story? As it turns out, kidnapping coverage in fairy tales is just as skewed as kidnapping coverage in modern day media.

NCE UPON ANOTHER TIME...

There lived a daring and intelligent young black woman named Jamila, who lived in the French countryside with her generous mother, tenacious father, and sweet younger brother. Jamila was captain of the town's archery team and currently had an apprenticeship with a gingerbread house architect.

While out for a jog one day, she took a new route and stumbled upon what she thought was a really beautiful botanical garden. Unfortunately, it was the front yard of a castle owned by a beast named Victor (formally known as Prince Victor Edward George Charles William Albert Henry John Phillip Archie VIII).

Victor Beast dragged Jamila back to his castle and locked her in a room in the dungeon. Typical basic beast shit.

"You can never return home!" he said, which seemed like an obvious point for a kidnapper to make.

After a few days of eating stale crumpets and drinking chalky water, Jamila was really hungry. Fortunately, a few of the household objects snuck down to the dungeon to bring Jamila some better food, including a bag of candy, a bottle of ketchup, and generic-brand potato chips. The Beast was a bachelor and his chef was currently a cheese grater so this was as good as it got.

Jamila befriended the objects, which included a Succulent (the former gardener), a Bar Cart (the former bartender), and a Doormat (a former door-to-door salesman named Mat who happened to be at the wrong place at the wrong time).

It was hard for the Bar Cart to stealthily sneak downstairs to visit Jamila since she was fully stocked and wheels and stairs don't go together. But luckily Victor Beast shaved his back hair every afternoon with an extremely loud Razor (the former barber), which gave the Bar Cart enough cover to bang down the stairs. Even though Victor was a gnarly beast, he was still a vain, prissy prince.

Jamila hoped someone would come and save her soon, but it was nice to have company while she waited.

Meanwhile, back in town, Jamila's family was desperate to bring attention to her kidnapping. But there was one problem: it was impossible to get the media on board.

The latest headlines from *Town Weekly, Good Morning Kingdom*, and *Pheasant and Friends* were about one woman and one woman only:

BELLE MISSING! UNRELATED: CHURCH BELL STOLEN!

WHAT REALLY HAPPENED TO THE BELLE OF THE BALL?

BEAUTY NO LONGER IN EYE OF THE BEHOLDER OR ANYONE ELSE FOR THAT MATTER! WHERE IS SHE?

"This is complete BS!" said Jamila's mother as she tossed the newspapers to the ground in frustration. "It's classic missing white woman syndrome. A cute, young, middle-class white lady goes missing and the media goes into a frenzy."

"Where's the coverage of our girl?" asked her father.

"Here's Jamila!" exclaimed her younger brother, pointing to a small sidebar in a tabloid called *Shooting Star*.

Jamila's father grabbed the issue and read the caption:

"Also missing: Jamila. Last seen out for a jog in tiny shorts and a sports bra. She was probably hanging with the wrong crowd and putting herself in danger. A source says she once befriended a gremlin."

"You've got to be kidding me!" yelled her mother. "Victim-blaming an innocent kidnapped woman?"

"That's it!" said her brother. "We're going down to the newsroom. Come on!"

Knock knock knock!

"What the hell?!" shouted Jamila's dad, once the editor opened the door. "You barely gave Jamila any coverage—or any of the missing women of color, for that matter!"

"Look, buddy, we cover what sells. I can't help it if people read what they want to read," said the editor.

"That's such a bullshit excuse," said her mother. "You are the media! It is your responsibility to tell people what's important. Giving these women less coverage reinforces a racial hierarchy and puts less pressure on authorities to solve the case."

"Ma'am, it's a tough industry. If I cover a story no one's interested in, the advertisers will flee. I can't help what people in the middle kingdom want to read."

"Have you ever considered that if you consistently cover more diverse stories, it would signal the importance of those stories and interest will follow?" challenged her father. "Or let me guess, none of your reporters want to cover the story, because you run a newsroom filled with white knights who only write about white nobles."

"Oh, come on! I can't fix a system-wide problem," he replied. "But since we're talking, any chance you know Belle's dad? Maybe from some parents of kidnapped children meetup or something? He won't talk to us but maybe you could get him to pay us a visit? Just need a quote or two!"

"Nope!" said Jamila's brother as he and his parents stormed out of the office and slammed the door.

Back at the castle, Jamila realized she needed to save herself. *Well, shit*, she thought.

"Hey, pals, any interest in being my accomplices and busting me out of here?" she asked her furniture friends one day. "I have a plan but I need your help."

"Heck yeah!" said the Succulent. "Our favorite story is 'Spellshank Redemption.' I'll start getting supplies!"

They began to collect the items she would need for the escape: a wooden spoon, 874 scarves, a pack of rubber bands, and some sticks. These were not the actual items Jamila wanted, but they were less suspicious versions of a shovel, a rope, and a bow and arrow.

Next, it was time for the furniture to begin training. They needed to get swole.

The Bar Cart practiced sprints along the castle hallways.

The Succulent pumped iron and drank plant protein.

And Mat, who had never swam in his life, began getting used to water by taking dunks in the guest room washbasin. After weeks of prep, the team was ready.

"Tomorrow, we ride," Jamila said.

The next day, Victor Beast started his daily back shave. Once she heard the sound of the Razor, Jamila gave the objects the signal: it was go time!

Jamila pushed her bed aside to reveal a tunnel she'd been digging with the wooden spoon. She crawled through the tunnel and out into the garden. She breathed in the fresh air and ducked behind a bush to catch her breath. She looked for her next move.

Jamila darted over to a nearby tree and scaled the trunk. Her plan was to quickly create a DIY zipline so she could sail over the castle gates to safety with the help of the Bar Cart. She tied the makeshift rope of 874 scarves to her bow and arrow made of sticks and rubber bands. Archery practice was about to pay off! She shot one arrow into the castle tower where the Bar Cart was waiting and another over the gates into a tree, stringing a long scarf zipline.

Jamila gave the signal to the Bar Cart.

"Bottoms up!" screamed the Bar Cart as she held on to her glassware and ziplined upside down on her wheels toward Jamila in the tree. "Wahooooo!"

But just as the Bar Cart was reaching Jamila to scoop her up and zipline over the gates to freedom, Victor Beast burst through the castle doors, galloping full speed toward the two of them in the tree. And the one thing beasts and basic bros at the gym never do is skip leg day.

But no worries—Jamila was prepared to hold him off! She reached into her pocket and pulled out the spiky extra limbs that the Succulent had grown. She chucked them at the Beast, spinning them like ninja stars. They sliced into the Beast's hairy arms, slowing him down ever so slightly. It was barely enough time for Jamila to get into the Bar Cart and sail over the Beast's head as they flew toward the castle gates.

They were about to clear the gates until one of the scarves came loose and the zipline SNAPPED! Jamila and the Bar Cart tumbled toward the ground. They looked behind them and there was the Beast—racing toward them.

"Run, run, run!" shouted the Bar Cart. "I got you!"

As Jamila scrambled for the gates, the Bar Cart steadied herself and tossed every shard of expensive glassware she still had on her at the Beast's head. One chunk of a heavy glass hit Victor Beast right between the eyes. The Beast went cross-eyed. Seeing ten Jamilas, he stumbled around, disoriented, not knowing which one to race after.

Jamila pulled herself over the gates using the broken zipline rope and sprinted until she reached the castle moat. *Crap!* The drawbridge she had jogged over months ago had been raised. But, no problem! She had a backup plan. She whipped out the Doormat from underneath her coat.

"Oh man, I was hoping Plan B wouldn't be necessary," Doormat Mat said, whimpering. "This is way scarier than a washbasin."

"You got this, Mat," Jamila said reassuringly.

He nodded.

Jamila threw him onto the moat's chilly water, stood on top of him, and used a nearby stick to paddleboard over the moat. And Mat didn't complain once. Because being a good ally means carrying your friends in their time of need—literally.

They made it to the other side and looked up. Jamila could see her village in the distance. She was free!

An hour after Jamila burst through the front door of her home and ran into her parents' arms, they still hadn't let go.

Soon her family got a chance to meet the Bar Cart and the Succulent when the rest of Victor Beast's furniture escaped through Jamila's tunnel. They furnished the entire town with fancy new luxurious goods. Except for the newsroom, which had to get by with unsightly, dated interiors. Victor Beast was cursed to live alone in his empty, furniture-less castle forever, with an incredibly hairy back.

Now, can you believe after all of that, the only kidnapping story you've heard is about a girl with Stockholm Syndrome who spent her time reading library books and playing in the snow with her captor?

Neither can we.

THE END

SOME PRINCESSES ARE GAY

NCE UPON A TIME...

There lived a prince who wanted to marry a princess. Also, his dad required him to marry a princess if he wanted to take over the successful family business of ruling the kingdom.

But it couldn't be just any princess from any rando kingdom. She needed to be smart, have great hair, and run a lifestyle blog. Finally, if the Prince was really getting serious with her, she had to undergo a special test. She had to prove she was delicate and sensitive enough to feel a single teeny tiny pea underneath twenty mattresses and twenty memory-foam pads.

There were many problems with this stupid test. For starters, being delicate and sensitive are not traits required for a male ruler. Also, blueberries would have smelled much nicer than peas. But, hey, this test had been passed from one royal generation to the next and no one ever questioned it.

The Prince chatted, swiped, and met a lot of princesses, but none who warranted a dinner date after a mead date. His parents were getting so concerned they had considered setting him up with the Queen's friend Sylvia's daughter even though she hadn't quite outgrown her goth phase.

One night, a terrible storm blew through the kingdom. Safe inside, the Prince sipped a mulled wine while playing games with a few squires when he heard a knock at the door. He rushed to the castle gates and there standing in the rain was a young woman.

"Can I please stay the night and wait out the storm?" she asked. "I'm a princess and I was on my way back to my kingdom when my horse got spooked by the lightning and ran off."

She peered inside and saw the squires.

"Are you all playing Dungeons and Dragons?" she exclaimed. "That is my favorite game! At my castle, we play in our actual dungeon with my pet dragon nearby because it feels festive."

They spent the evening playing various games, discussing where they went to finishing school, and listening to their favorite indie wizard bands that could simultaneously cast spells and shred on the mandolin.

The Prince couldn't believe his luck! The Princess was funny, smart, and he enjoyed her company. The King and Queen, who had been subtly listening in from the next room, could barely contain their excitement.

"Don't mind us!" said the Queen as she burst through the door with a bowl of turkey leg snacks so she could get a better look at the Princess. "We thought you two might want something to munch on."

"Hey, squires, take a hint and skedaddle," said the King.

The Princess appeared to check off all of the boxes. Even after getting caught in a storm, she still had great hair. Anyone who could beat the Prince at so many games clearly had a brain, and a quick search revealed her popular lifestyle blog, called *The Twig*, which she posted on a scroll outside her castle each morning. She was perfect!

It was time for the pea test. The King and Queen placed a tiny pea on the bottom of a guest room bed, gathered twenty mattresses and twenty memory-foam pads from around the castle, and piled them on top. They hoped the Princess would have as much of a hard time sleeping tonight as they would waiting for the results.

The Prince and Princess said goodnight to each other and parted for their separate rooms. The Princess thought it was extremely bizarre that she needed to climb an extension ladder to get to the top of her bed but figured maybe that was just what they considered chic interior design in this kingdom. Either that or they had a roach problem.

In the morning, the family gathered in the dining hall and waited for the Princess to awaken. Would she pass the pea test? Was she so refined as to feel a single pea underneath twenty mattresses and twenty memory-foam pads? Was she "the one?"

Finally the Princess walked into the room. She had bags under her eyes and yawned widely.

"Is coffee a thing in this kingdom? If so, I'd love a quadruple espresso."

"I take it you didn't sleep well?" the Queen asked giddily.

"Was there anything wrong with your bed?" asked the King.

Normally she wouldn't have complained, but maybe they wanted genuine feedback on their strangely tall beds.

"You would think a lot of cushion would be comfortable but to be honest, it felt like there was a giant rock stabbing me in my back all night," said the Princess.

"Hooray!" said the Prince. "You passed the test! We put a pea under your bed to see if you would feel it. And you did! Will you marry me?"

"At least there's not a roach problem. Also, no. I'm gay."

"Really?" said the Prince.

"Yep. I am very much attracted to women. Mostly, brown eyes with cheekbones that can slice a stone," said the Princess. "This isn't, like, something I'm making up to get out of marrying you."

"You can't be gay, you seem so normal," said the King.

"I am normal. You're the one who stacks forty mattresses on top of each other."

"But you could feel the pea!" said the Queen. "That means you're delicate and sensitive, like all the straight princesses I know. Except for Sylvia's goth tragedy of a daughter."

"Whoa. What exactly do you think lesbian princesses are like?" said the Princess, scrunching her forehead.

"The way you asked that question makes me think maybe I shouldn't answer it," said the Queen.

"How do you know you like women?" asked the King.

"I've just always known," explained the Princess patiently. She'd been through this before.

"But … how?" repeated the King.

"The same way I know you put a pea under my mattresses last night," said the Princess. "It's obvious."

"But if you've never been with a prince, how do you know you wouldn't like it?" asked the Queen.

"Do you need to kiss a frog to know you don't want to kiss a frog?" asked the Princess.

"Well, actually, my cousin kissed a frog and it worked out great for her," said the Prince.

"I heard about that. Bad example," said the Princess. "My point is, I know I don't want to kiss a prince."

"But who will you pass your crown on to?" asked the King. "Royal legacy can't end because you're into chicks."

"If I meet another princess I dig, I can marry her, rule the land, and when we're ready, we'll figure out how to have a family if we want. There are a lot of options and different kinds of families."

"Hm. It's strange we've never thought about that as an option," said the Queen.

"Indeed it is," said the King. "I suppose we've just never met a gay princess before."

"Or you didn't realize it," said the Princess. "A lot of people assume it's not hard to be gay anymore because it's so accepted in pop culture thanks to *Modern Royal Family*, but discrimination and violence toward gay people still exists."

"Thank you for explaining all this to my parents," said the Prince. "Before you head home can we play one more game of Dungeons and Dragons? We could also listen to the new album from Sorcerer Youth."

"Totally. But one last thing. You all gotta get rid of the pea thing," said the Princess. "I almost fell off the bed a few times. It's super dangerous. And the only thing that test actually reveals is what a whiny house guest someone is to complain about the guest bed."

"Come to think of it, why can't I just rule the kingdom on my own?" said the Prince.

"It's strange we've never thought about that as an option either," said the King. "I guess you can! We just assumed happiness was a retread of our own life and how we lived. The pea test worked for us. We've been married forty-seven years!"

"I never felt the pea," the Queen said quietly.

"What?!" said the King.

"I had a huge crush on you and bribed one of the ladies in waiting to tell me about the test," said the Queen. "But it all worked out, right?"

"Indeed it did," said the King.

From that day forth, future female leaders were tested for their integrity, intelligence, and taste in music, the Queen gave the extension ladder back to the fire department, and the only thing peas were used for was soup.

THE END

UNDER NOBODY'S THUMB

NCE UPON A TIME...

There lived an adventurous and charming young woman named Thumbelina who was single and liked to mingle. She was a capital "I" Independent woman. She was a very little lady about town. How little, you ask? Let us explain.

There was an old woman who lived on her own in a cottage in one of those small artsy towns that retired single ladies like to live in two hours away from a major city. She longed for a child, so she decided to call up the local witch. She heard magic spells were easier than IVF.

The witch gave her a piece of barley corn and told her to plant it.

"I guess the witch wants to see if I can keep a flower alive before I keep a human alive," said the woman to herself, worriedly looking over at all of her dead ferns.

Despite her concerns, she watered the plant studiously and one day it bloomed. When it opened, a young woman the size of a thumb was sitting inside of the flower.

"I will call you Thumbelina," said the woman, whose own name was Lampina, because she was the size of her parents' floor lamp and assumed that's how you named people.

Thumbelina was magically born as a young adult, and while it's a shame she missed her early childhood, on the bright side she was able to skip over the worst parts of puberty. While most people who miss their childhood usually end up filling the void with drugs and paparazzi, Thumbelina had a grounded life full of singing, gardening, and sleeping in a tiny walnut shell.

Just like her mother, Thumbelina had no interest in settling down.

All of Thumbelina's besties were frogs since it was easier to share clothes with creatures her own size. The frogs loved Thumbelina's wild dating stories at brunch, but if they were being honest, they felt like it was time for her to pick a sig other instead of jumping from log to log.

One evening, they decided to intervene. While Thumbelina was fast asleep in her walnut shell, her frog friends kidnapped her to introduce her to one of their respectable single friends, a toad named Toady McToad.

"We're setting you up on a blind date. So fun!" exclaimed one of the frogs. "He's single, he wants to settle down and he only has two warts."

"Girls, you know I love a good setup, but I have no interest in meeting Toady McToad or anyone looking to lock me down," said Thumbelina. "I am happy dating around and hooking up with whomever I want. I'm safe, I feel empowered, and I know the best shared appetizer at every restaurant."

"But if you fall in love with Toady, we can all go on group dates and you don't have to be a fifth wheel all of the time," croaked one of the friends. "It makes us uncomfortable and sad. For you."

"That's your projection, because I've never had a problem being a third wheel or fifth wheel or any wheel," said Thumbelina.

"Toady McToad is a great toad," said one of the friends. "He's funny and he isn't like one of those fuckboys you usually date."

"Wow. Yes, I am into fuckboys. But you said you loved my stories about the raccoon who lived in that oak tree penthouse and the beetle who invited me on tour with him. I do not appreciate you slut-shaming me," said Thumbelina.

She hopped on a lily pad nearby, flashed her friends a peace sign, and began floating downstream. "Peace out, jerks."

"You'll thank us when you stop amplexusing around!" they croaked after her. "That's a frog mating position, by the way!"

The current was strong, and soon Thumbelina was miles away from home. She steered her lily pad over to the side of the river and began looking for shelter, but she was deep in the woods. This was worse than the time she forgot to book a hotel on vacation and ended up crashing in a squirrel's nest with nest bugs.

Soon she came upon a tiny door in a tree stump and knocked, forgetting everything her mother had told her about stranger danger. The door swung open and there stood a mouse.

"Oh my! Come inside you poor little thing, you must be starving," said the mouse, who introduced herself as Aunty Mouse.

Thumbelina was grateful for the food and warmth, while Aunty Mouse was grateful to have someone to show off her craft room to, where she bedazzled fanny packs to sell at the market.

After a few days, though, Aunty Mouse started pestering Thumbelina about her single status. Like any normal aunt, the three things she was best at were gifting clothes from the 80s, making deviled eggs, and getting way too invested in someone's dating life.

"I don't get it," she said, "You're pretty and smart and you can see color. Humans and animals alike should be falling in love with you!"

"I enjoy being single," said Thumbelina. "I like to sleep like a starfish, I like peeing with the door open, I like knowing my leftovers will still be in the fridge and I like binge-reading fables without having to wait for someone."

Aunty Mouse didn't accept Thumbelina's explanation because of a time-honored convention: a single woman can't possibly know what's best for her. The next night, Aunty Mouse invited a guest over for dinner.

"Oh, Mr. Mole! What a pleasant surprise," said Aunty Mouse, doing a terrible job of feigning shock.

"You invited me," said Mr. Mole. "You said, 'I have a really hot little lady staying at my house who I want you to meet.' And while moles can only see light and movement, I still like the idea of dating someone hot."

"Anyway, Thumbelina, meet Mr. Mole. He has a great velvet jacket and everyone knows only cultured and cool people wear fancy velvet jackets. I think you guys will hit it off, and who knows? Maybe one day you will get married and end Thumbelina's extremely sad, lonesome existence."

"We're both unmarried, so why do you think this mole guy—who is two decades older than me—is independent and sophisticated, while I'm desperate and lonely?" said Thumbelina.

"It's just different," said Aunty Mouse. "He's a silver fox-mole, and you're almost past your prime."

Mr. Mole spent the next two insufferable hours discussing his art collection, the renovation on his summer molehill, and why he loves sweet potatoes.

"Whelp, I hate sweet potatoes and I don't value my self-worth based on whether or not I'm in a relationship, so this won't work out," said Thumbelina.

When Mr. Mole left, Thumbelina curled up in her bed and started crying. She wanted to leave Aunty Mouse's single-shamey house with bad shower pressure, but she was too far to make the journey on her own.

A sparrow who was eating berries nearby and had overheard the disaster of a date flew down.

"Girl, you deserve better than that loser mole and nosy mouse," chirped the Sparrow. "Sparrows mate for life but we don't judge birds or mammals who don't."

"This is very validating," said Thumbelina.

"Let's get you outta here. Hop on my back, Thumbelina, and I'll fly you home!"

Thumbelina climbed on the Sparrow's back and held on tight to her feathers while they flew high above the forest. Midway through the trip, the Sparrow stopped for a pee break in a flower garden. The bird thought it was messed up to piss on people while flying.

While Thumbelina waited, a small man flew out from behind a rose bush. He was Thumbelina's size but had a pair of wings on his back. He was a prince (shocker)!

"Do you believe in love at first sight?" the Fairy Prince asked, winking. "Or should I fly past you again?"

"Excuse me?"

"I'm the Fairy Prince and I have already decided I want to marry you!"

"I'm Thumbelina, and I have already decided that will never happen," said Thumbelina. "First of all, you literally just met me and second of all, what is it with everyone trying to marry me lately? A toad, a mole, and now you!"

"Of course you wouldn't want to marry a toad or a mole. That's gross. But I am a Fairy Prince with a supremely stylish, high and tight fade haircut."

"Look, buddy. I don't ever want to get married," said Thumbelina.

"Why not?" asked the Prince.

"Do you really want me to get into it?" asked Thumbelina.

"Hit me with it!" said the Fairy Prince.

Thumbelina took a deep breath.

"Marriage is an outdated patriarchal institution that is rooted in economic alliances and toxic gender roles that saw women as the property of their fathers and then husbands," said Thumbelina. "Also, I hate cake."

"Yikes!" said the Prince. "Now I feel kinda bad that I've dreamed of getting married my whole life. I've already sketched out the perfect tuxedo to wear—it will be periwinkle!"

"And you will look great. I absolutely don't judge people or animals who want to get married—and to be clear, all creatures should have the right to get married—it's just not something I want," said Thumbelina. "But for some reason, everyone in my life seems to think this is a problem."

"I can't wait to get married," said the Fairy Prince. "Royal fairy weddings are great for ratings."

"I love a good royal fairy wedding. I have a commemorative mug from the last one," said Thumbelina. "What I don't love is long-term monogamy. Even if that changes down the road, I don't need the government to approve of my relationship for it to be considered valid."

"Can't say I didn't try!" said the Prince. "Farewell my beautiful, proudly promiscuous, and independent Thumbelina."

"Farewell my Fairy Prince," said Thumbelina. "If you have a good vegan option, don't forget to invite me to your wedding!"

And with that, the Sparrow scooped up Thumbelina and flew her home where she lived happily single ever after.

THE END

@THEREALGOLDILOCKS &
#THETHREEBEARS

NCE UPON A TIME...

There lived a loving family of three bears: a Mama Bear, a Papa Bear, and a Baby Bear. Every day they woke up and made porridge, which is like if oatmeal and grits had a breakfast baby. They always put the porridge in the microwave for a minute too long. Half of the time it exploded and they had to clean the microwave. The other half of the time they would go for a walk while it cooled on the kitchen table.

One morning while they were on their porridge-cooling walk, a young girl named Goldilocks spotted the Bears' home as she was posing in front of a graffiti wall nearby. She was on the hunt to take some fierce pics for her social. She peeked inside and thought their home would be the perfect backdrop for a faux-candid photo series.

"This house is presh! So much character. It's just what I need!"

Without thinking twice, she turned the knob of the front door and let herself in, because no one had ever told her no as a child.

"Hello!" she called out. "My name is Goldilocks. I'm here to take pictures in your home. I have a lot of followers and I'm going to blow this home up on the internet."

Nobody answered, so Goldilocks shrugged and started snapping away. She pulled out her phone tripod and selfie light to get some photos of herself posing in various places around the Bears' supes cute home.

She posed in front of the entryway gallery wall featuring generations of the Bears' family that she thought gave off major ski chalet vibes. She put her hands on her hips, jutted her collarbones forward and turned her good side toward the camera. Next, she stood in front of the fireplace, and pretended to warm her hands while serving the camera some 'tude.

Then she spotted the porridge cooling down on the kitchen table.

"This porridge is perfect for my breakfast post!" she exclaimed, examining the quirky ceramic bowls it was plated in. "I'll add some flowers around the bowls to give it some zhuzh."

She snapped a photo of herself with the porridges and then looked for the perfect filter.

"This filter is too hot," she said as she swiped through different options. "This filter is too cold. But this filter is just right!"

She figured she ought to taste the porridge to write an authentic caption. Plus, she was hungry. So she gulped down Baby Bear's porridge.

"Made myself some tasty and healthy cinnamon coconut goodness for brekkie," Goldilocks typed into the caption field.

Next she went into the living room, where she spotted three velvet arm chairs lined up in a row.

"These chairs look like they're straight out of the Restoration HardBear catalogue!" squealed Goldilocks. "I've gotta get some photos in them."

First, she posed in Papa Bear's chair, but it was too wide and the proportions were all off. Next she tried Mama Bear's chair, but it was too narrow and she looked awkward in it. Then, she tried Baby Bear's chair, and it was just right. She kneeled on the chair's cushion and struck a pose. But after she snapped the photo, she heard a loud tear as the upholstery split and her leg pierced through the center!

"This chair is busted. Whoops," she said. "I bet they're RHB knock-offs anyway. It's the chair's fault. Stupid chair."

She was ready to pack up and head out but remembered she needed to post some sponsored content. That's when she spotted a staircase leading up to the Bears' bedroom. She climbed the stairs and swung the door open. Inside were three charming wooden country beds she thought were totally cottage chic.

She jumped onto Papa Bear's bed, never questioning whether this was an invasion of privacy. She landed with a thud.

"Hey there G-Squad! OMG, look at this guy's bed. Rock. Hard," she vlogged to her followers. "He could really use some softer linens. Use promocode GOLDEN at StorytimeBeds.com so you don't end up like this old geezer."

Next she tried Mama Bear's bed, but it was too soft.

"G-Squad, who can even sleep like this? This bed is so soft. Watch what happens when I try to take a photo. I sink into the bed and it covers up this fab mesh top–skirt combo. Cute skirt though, right? Get this look at FairyApparel.com by using promocode GOLDIGURL."

Lastly she tried Baby Bear's bed and it was just right. She sprawled herself across the bed, when she began to get sleepy.

"I worked so hard today, G-Squad," said Goldilocks to her followers. "Photoshoots can be really exhausting. I never have time to run errands, like going to the post office. Use promocode YELLOWHAIR at Stamps.com."

She promptly fell fast asleep in Baby Bear's bed.

Meanwhile, the Bears had finished their breakfast stroll and were eager to eat their porridge. They opened up their front door and immediately realized something was off.

They looked at the kitchen table and saw the flowers around their porridge bowls.

"Somebody has been photographing my porridge!" said Papa Bear.

"Somebody has been photographing my porridge!" said Mama Bear.

"Somebody has been photographing my porridge, and they ate it all up!" said Baby Bear.

Realizing there had been an intruder, they began to look around their home. The gallery wall photos were tilted, the pillows on their living room chairs were completely thrown about, and there was a phone tripod on the coffee table.

"Somebody has been posing in my chair!" said Papa Bear.

"Somebody has been posing in my chair!" said Mama Bear.

"Somebody has been posing in my chair, and they split the cushion open!" said Baby Bear.

Just then, Papa Bear spotted the door at the top of the stairs cracked open. They climbed the stairs and peered inside their bedroom. Papa Bear's oversized pillows had been tossed on the ground, Mama Bear's homemade quilt had been thrown on the floor, and there was a selfie light on the nightstand table.

"Somebody has been vlogging in my bed!" said Papa Bear.

"Somebody has been vlogging in my bed!" said Mama Bear.

"Somebody has been vlogging in my bed, and they're still there!" said Baby Bear.

The Bears let out a yelp of surprise.

Goldilocks jolted awake. Her eyes went wide when she saw the three bears standing over her.

"Call the authorities!" shouted Mama Bear.

"Wait!" said Goldilocks. "Do you know who I am?"

"No, that's the whole problem. We don't know who you are," said Papa Bear.

"And you're in my bed," said Baby Bear.

"I'm a very popular influencer who just conducted a major photo sesh in your home. You should be happy to have me here. This photo sesh was kismet."

"You let yourself into our home without asking," said Papa Bear.

"Yeah, but it was for the pics, and I needed them," responded Goldilocks.

"Do you know how that sounds?" asked Mama Bear.

"No," said Goldilocks.

"Entitled."

"My title?" said Goldilocks. "I'm @therealgoldilocks. The handle @goldilocks was already taken and that B wouldn't sell it to me."

"'Entitled' means you only think about yourself and believe you deserve special treatment and privileges," said Baby Bear. "And that you eat other people's breakfast because you think you can have whatever you want."

"Listen. You're not hearing me. I've taken a bunch of hella sweet pics of your house. I made it look way better than it actually looks IRL. These posts will be very popular. You should be thanking me. What are you? One of those people who hates social media?"

"As it turns out, I'm actually a very popular Mommy Bear blogger. This isn't about the photos, it's about your lack of respect for other people," said Mama Bear. "You broke and entered our house without permission and feel zero remorse about going through our stuff. What part of you thinks that's okay?"

"The part that already has 1,432 likes on this post," said Goldilocks, holding up her phone.

"I've met a lot of privileged jerks in my life, but not one as young as you," said Mama Bear.

"Thank you!" said Goldilocks.

"This girl is the worst," said Baby Bear.

As Papa Bear called the authorities to report her for breaking and entering, Goldilocks ran toward the bedroom window. But as she prepared to jump out and get away, she noticed the sun was casting incredible light. She pulled out her phone for one last photo, but as she did, she slipped. She fell out of the window, landed badly, and broke her neck.

We know what you're thinking: having someone break their neck and end up in the hospital because they're an entitled narcissist and ate someone's brekkie is a little extreme. But we didn't even make that up! It's part of the original story. And no, a prince did not come to save her.

We guess this is one situation where the classic fairy tale wasn't so bad after all.

THE END

ACKNOWLEDGMENTS

To our fairy godmother book agent Cindy Uh. We are grateful to have someone as fierce as you in our corner. Also, thank you for telling us that our book proposal needed to have "professional photos" of us instead of the ones of us dressed as princesses.

To Stephanie Knapp, Laura Mazer, Kaitlin Carruthers-Busser, and the team at Seal Press for publishing this book, supporting us along the way, and staying true to our voice. You have to kiss a lot of frog editors until you find princess ones.

To the Upright Citizens Brigade Theatre, Shannon O'Neill, Bridget Holmes, Michael Hartney, and the entire crew at UCB Hell's Kitchen. Thank you for the opportunity to perform our sketch show that became this book and for allowing us to spit out a condom on your stage in the name of comedy.

To Madalyn Baldanzi. Thank you for encouraging us to keep going with this idea and pitching jokes such as "I don't want to hurt the lips with the pulling."

To Amber Reauchean Williams for being the best castmate and friend we could ask for and for making our words even funnier onstage. Thanks for trying to fix that cheap-ass Rapunzel wig we bought on Amazon so many times.

To our directors Chet Siegel and Matt Gehring for bringing our sketches to life, including a choreographed dance to the song "A Woke New World." Matt, we're still mad you cut Nana dog from the Tinker Bell sketch.

To Armando Zubieta for taking photos of us dressed as princesses with pussy hats and not asking for an explanation. To Jackie Abbott for both your notes and tolerating the cold to take photos of us in crowns and business suits, which the hipsters in Brooklyn thought was just "our look." We are beyond grateful to you both for your talents and generosity.

To Disney for giving us our love of fairy tales, even though you wrote lines like "leave the sewing to the women" and "girls talk too much." You're getting better. To the Brothers Grimm for sneaking in some R-rated violence and gore into children's tales. And to Hans Christian Andersen for being a total weirdo.

To our friends and family who gave us invaluable feedback or supported the project along the way: Lauren Adams, Monica Bergstrand, Jen Birn, Mallory Blair, Ben Blake, Matt Cody, Cristina Cote, J. W. Crump, Nicole Drespel, Whitney English, Hampton Fluker, Cora Frazier, Sam French, Cristina Gibson, Betty Gilpin, Molly Griggs, Sarah Houghton, Rich and Ella Johnston, Samia Khan, Jess Keefe, Alex Keegan, Sally Langlitz, Reagan Lopez, Amanda Champagne Meadows, Sarah Merrill, Darla Murray, Jensen Olaya, Eloise Parker, Mary Beth Quirk, Bre Racano, Sue and Denny Radkowsky, Evan Real, Franses Rodriguez, Ali Schwartz, Angela Spera, Matt Sullivan, Abe Tabaie, Dayane Taylor, Laura Willcox, and Jay Wolff.

To our parents, Amy, Andy, Bill, and Lindy. Thank you for sitting through the many, many hours of unrehearsed living-room productions of fairy tales as children. Who could have guessed those were first drafts of a show we'd write, produce, and act in in our 30s? We love you.

To our younger siblings Jonathan, Molly, Grace, and Polly for letting us dress you up and "play princess." We love you, too.

To Samo the dog for being so chill during rehearsals and book writing meetings and giving us emotional support in the form of licking our feet.

To Nic for being my personal show photographer, graphic designer, and first draft reader. Thank you for our son and for our life. I don't believe women need a Prince Charming but if I did, you're pretty close to it.

To Dru for trekking to Hell's Kitchen Theatre to drop off postcards for the show, for delaying our honeymoon for this book's deadline, and for being better than happily ever after (which doesn't exist, but, you get it).

Thank you to the feminist icons and thinkers everywhere and the people on the frontlines trying to make the world a more equal place. You continue to teach us. Don't let the comment section drive you mad.

LAURA LANE is a comedy writer, podcaster, performer, and author. She's written for *People, McSweeney's*, the Belladonna, the *New Yorker*, ESPN, *Esquire, Vanity Fair*, and *Cosmopolitan*. Previously she was an entertainment magazine editor. The sketch show and book she co-wrote called *This Is Why You're Single* was optioned for TV and has been covered by the *New York Times*, the *Washington Post*, and the *Wall Street Journal*.

ELLEN HAUN is a writer, actor, and comedian. She played the hapless law student Ms. Chapin on ABC's *How to Get Away with Murder*. Ellen co-wrote and starred in the web series *OMGHI* and the short film *No Limes*. She has performed at the Sydney Opera House, Williamstown Theatre Festival, and Actors Theatre of Louisville. She is a regular performer at the Peoples Improv Theater and the Upright Citizens Brigade Theatre.

ABOUT THE ILLUSTRATOR

Nicole Miles is an illustrator based in the United Kingdom.